Knox County Tennessee

A History in Pictures

BETSEY BEELER CREEKMORE

Betsey B. Creekmore

This book is one of
a limited edition of 2,500

Teacher, journalist, and American naturalist John Burroughs had a way with words. "Time," he wrote, "does not become sacred to us until we have lived with it, until it has passed over us and taken with it a part of ourselves."

Betsey Beeler Creekmore brings that message to home and heart in *Knox County: A History in Pictures*. This limited collector's edition is a stunning preservation of the people, places, and traditions that have shaped the heart of Tennessee's Resource Valley into what it is today...and foreshadows what we will become tomorrow.

Bank Of East Tennessee and the News Sentinel Company feel proud and privileged to play a part in this worthy undertaking. For over a century, the News Sentinel Company has been entrusted by this community to record, document, and shed light on the events of our times and how they affect each of us. Though a relative newcomer, Bank Of East Tennessee has been entrusted with a growing share of the financial wealth of this community and has answered its call to contribute also through projects such as this to the civic and cultural wealth of our Resource Valley. Together, we offer a firmly clasped handshake in agreement and in endorsement of this richly moving and thoroughly enjoyable recollection.

Proceeds from this endeavor are earmarked for the endowment funds of the Blount Mansion Association and the University of Tennessee Library System. What better way to pay tribute to our home than to appreciate and support the many unique assets which allow us to cherish this very special "part of ourselves."

KNOXVILLE NEWS SENTINEL COMPANY
A SCRIPPS HOWARD COMPANY

Bank Of East Tennessee
Member FDIC

Knox County Tennessee
A History in Pictures

Betsey Beeler Creekmore

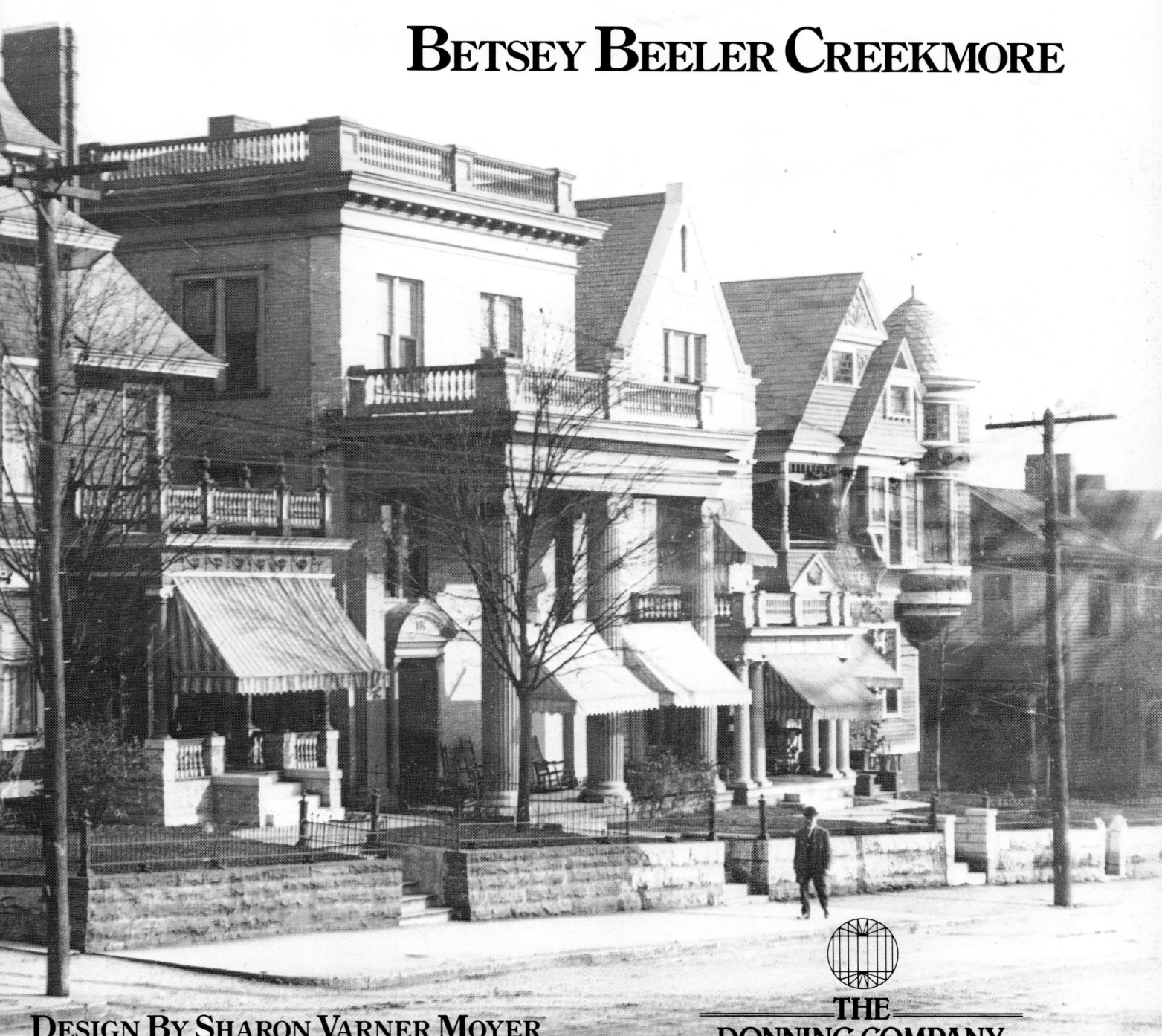

Design By Sharon Varner Moyer

THE DONNING COMPANY
PUBLISHERS
NORFOLK/VIRGINIA BEACH

The Donning Company/Publishers
Norfolk/Virginia Beach

Copyright © 1988 by Betsey Beeler Creekmore
All rights reserved, including the right to reproduce this work in any form whatsoever without permission in writing from the publisher, except for brief passages in connection with a review. For information, write:

The Donning Company/Publishers
5659 Virginia Beach Boulevard
Norfolk, Virginia 23502

Edited by Kevin Mitchelle Johnson
Richard A. Horwege, Senior Editor

Library of Congress Cataloging-in-Publication Data

Creekmore, Betsey Beeler.
   Knox County, Tennessee: a history in pictures/
by Betsey Beeler Creekmore.
   p.   cm.
   Bibliography: p.
   Includes index.
   ISBN 0-89865-731-8
   1. Knox County (Tenn.)—History—Pictorial works. 2. Knox County (Tenn.)—Description and travel—Views. I. Title.
F457.K6C74   1988
976.8'85'00222—dc19   88-23734
                                               CIP

Printed in the United States of America

CONTENTS

Foreword 7

Acknowledgments 9

Introduction 11
    How Knox County Came To Be

Chapter 1 19
    East Knox County

Chapter 2 53
    South Knox County

Chapter 3 85
    North Knox County

Chapter 4 118
    West Knox County

Chapter 5 147
    A City Within The City—
    The University of Tennessee

Chapter 6 165
    Knoxville—The County Seat

Bibliography 236

Index 237

About The Author 240

FOREWORD

She says, "I'm not an historian. Doesn't matter to me if it happened on Tuesday or Wednesday. I'm interested in the *story*. I hope people will want to read through the captions—almost without looking at the pictures—and *there* will be the story of Knox County."

I have read through the captions the way Betsey Creekmore suggested (although it is impossible to resist the pictures). It is a pleasant journey led by an author whose enthusiasm for her hometown (she originated the Dogwood Trails in 1955) and scholarship (eleven books, including two local histories) already have earned for her the rank of number one storyteller of the history of Knoxville and Knox County.

What is most interesting is how Betsey's book reminds us of what still is left of old Knox County, how much of it is downtown and in Hardin Valley and in the turn-of-the century Fourth and Gill neighborhood, for instance. She chronicles the beginnings of the University of Tennessee in 1794, and how trees chopped down before the Civil War Battle of Fort Sanders never grew back and the hillside stayed bare until a hospital opened there in the 1920s. I enjoyed the familiar photographs showing the creation of the Great Smoky Mountains National Park and the Tennessee Valley Authority, and I was pleased to learn that in 1913 Knoxville was home for the first National Conservation Exposition.

Knowing all these things about one's hometown seems to be more important these days. Now, historians aren't the only ones interested. I think this is because people are grasping for ways to deal with the enormous change of this rushing world. After suffering enough of this change, more of us are deciding that the best way to live is not to keep letting change run over us but to find a way to take it on our own terms—and the best way to start doing that is to pause to think about what in our lives is worth holding onto. Betsey Creekmore's story is a fine way for anyone who cares about Knoxville and Knox County to rediscover what in this hometown there is— and there is a lot—worth holding onto.

Lamar Alexander
President, The University of Tennessee
Knoxville

July 1, 1988

Acknowledgments

I am deeply grateful to these friends, who have shared their treasured family photographs, their wealth of knowledge, and—most valuable of all—their time: Lamar Alexander; John M. Armistead; Cheryl Bartley; Barbara Winick Bernstein; Isabel Ashe Bonnyman; Margaret Singleton Carson; David D. Creekmore; Katie Morrell Dalton; Linda Davidson; Joseph Delaney; Harold Diftler; Ralph Diggs; Hal Ernest; Mary Thomas Fleury; Helen Brownlow Fritts; LeRoy P. Graf; Elizabeth Price Heinsohn; C. Milton Hinshilwood; Jack Kirkland; Margaret Maxey Latham; Hardy Liston, Jr.; Howard Lumsden; Cecil Holloway Matheny; Robert L. McClure; Betty Jean Hay McNair; Mark Mitchum; Juliana Nickerson; Jack E. Reese; Ernest B. Robertson, Jr.; Peggy Briscoe Rochelle; Nancy McMillan Rodgers; Anne Lee Spaugh Smith; Mitchell Taylor; Anne Henegar Thomas; Rodman Townsend; and Zona Whitson.

Photographs from the following collections were generously made available: McClung Historical Collection—Steve Cotham and Sally Ripatti; UT Center for Educational Video and Photography—Ernest B. Robertson, Jr., and Nick Myers; UTK Special Collections Library—John Dobson and Steven Wicks; Blount Mansion Association—Kent Whitworth; *Knoxville News-Sentinel* Library—Shirley Carter; Metropolitan Planning Commission, Historic Buildings Survey—Ann Bennett and Chris Wood; Greater Knoxville Chamber of Commerce—Darrell Akins; Tennessee Valley Authority—Charles H. Dean; Dogwood Arts Festival—Jim Walls; Beck Cultural Exchange Center—Rev. Lea Earl Acuff and Margaret Carson; Knoxville Convention and Visitors Bureau—Al Treadaway; Knoxville Heritage, Inc.—Nancy Brown; East Tennessee Community Design Center—Annette Andersen; Knoxville College Archives—Patty Cooper; Frank H. McClung Museum—Elaine Evans; City of Knoxville, Office of Information—Sue Clancy; Knox County Schools Professional Library—Elizabeth Hotchkiss and Marjorie Rogers; Public Building Authority of Knox County—Michael Edwards; Students' Museum, Inc.—David Sincerbox; Knaffl and Brakebill, Photographers—Sam Knaffl, Jr.; Tracy Photography—Ernest Tracy; and *Knoxville Journal* negative files, in the McClung Historical Collection.

Information was also provided, through conversations or publications, by: East Tennessee Historical Society; Knox County Chapter, Association for the Preservation of Tennessee Antiquities; Chapter 89, United Daughters of the Confederacy; Bonny Kate Chapter, Daughters of the American Revolution; James White Chapter, Daughters of the American Revolution; Simon Harris Chapter, Daughters of the American Revolution; Lawson McGhee Library; Appalachian Zoological Society; James White's Fort Association; Ossoli Circle; K-Trans; U.S. Constitution Bicentennial Committee of Knoxville and Knox County; Knoxville Garden Club; Arnstein Jewish Community Center; Junior League of Knoxville, Main Street, Knoxville, Inc.; Knoxville Police Department; Knoxville/Knox County Homecoming '86 Steering Committee; and Knoxville/Knox County U.S. Constitution Bicentennial Committee.

New Photographs were taken especially for this book by: Roy Buckner; Gary Heatherly; Jack Kirkland; Nick Myers; Ernest B. Robertson, Jr.; and Miles Wright.

In such a project, there is invariably a "person without whom." As courier, critic, and computer expert, my daughter, Betsey Creekmore has been the indispensible volunteer.

—Betsey Beeler Creekmore

The Cherokee claimed East Tennessee as their traditional hunting grounds for deer and buffalo, which still roamed the valleys when the first white settlers came. Drawing from History of Tennessee *by Gentry R. McGee*

Introduction

How Knox County Came To Be

The settlement of Knox County began in 1785.
Surely that can't be right! How could a part of North Carolina, where England's first New World colony was established by Sir Walter Raleigh in 1584, remain uninhabited for two hundred years?

Ah, but that's the point. It wasn't uninhabited.

Archeologists sifting the soil of East Tennessee's Indian mounds and village sites have unearthed evidence of occupation and conquest spanning more than fifteen hundred years. First came the Woodland Indians, fierce hunters who roamed primeval forests that abounded with elk and bear. They were driven out by the Mound Builders, valley dwellers who not only hunted deer and buffalo, but planted corn. These early Mississippian Indians were displaced in turn by the Cherokee, who were akin in language and customs to the Iroquois.

The Cherokee were not a nomadic tribe, but a powerful nation. Long before the first white explorers set foot in East Tennessee, they had built a series of towns beside the Little Tennessee River; and there they enjoyed an enviable lifestyle. They were well housed in large round structures like inverted baskets, made by interweaving stout posts with pliant saplings. They varied their diet of wild game and fish with the produce of cornfields and vegetable gardens, and they were comfortably clad in supple deerskin, with rich furs for winter overcoats and blankets. They also rejoiced in a democratic form of government, in which each man (and some women) had a voice. In only one respect could the Cherokee have been called backward: They were all illiterate, because they had no written language.

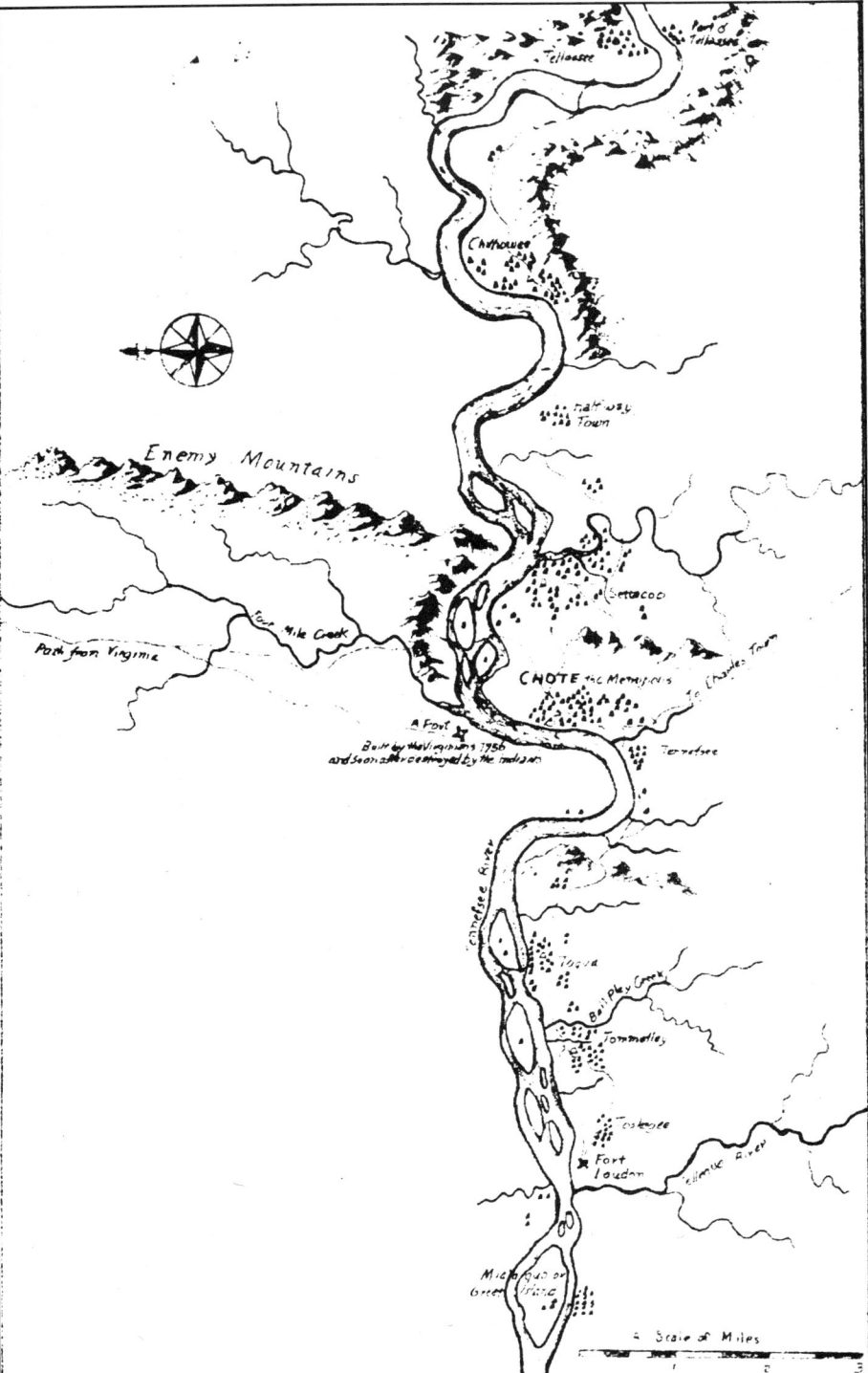

Lt. Henry Timberlake of the British army passed through future Knox County in 1762 during his exploration of the western wilderness. After his return to civilization, he published this map of the Cherokee settlements along the Little Tennessee River in his Memoirs.

In theory, the British Colony of North Carolina extended from the Atlantic Ocean to the Mississippi River, but half of this territory lay beyond towering mountains covered with inpenetrable forests; therefore, the population spread westward from the coastal plain to the Piedmont region, and stopped. There was no way to get here from there.

Beginning in 1673, East Tennessee's earliest explorers bypassed the mountains by following Indian trails from South Carolina and Virginia. Returning travellers glowingly described the transmontane country as a land of broad rivers, fertile valleys, and upland forests teeming with wild game of every kind, BUT, they warned, it was the home of the strong, shrewd Cherokee who had no wish to sell or share it.

During the French and Indian Wars, the Cherokee allied themselves with the English, who promised to build a fort at the mouth of the Little Tennessee River, and send a garrison of soldiers to protect the nearby towns. Red-coated troops followed the Indian trail from South Carolina in 1756, and constructed an elaborate, diamond-shaped earthworks stronghold named in honor of the Earl

Restored Fort Loudoun is not situated beside the TVA lake that bears its name, but on a promontory overlooking nearby Tellico Lake. Tennessee Valley Authority

of Loudoun who was commander-in-chief of all British forces in North America at the time. The Cherokee were vastly entertained by the bustle of construction at Fort Loudoun, but they soon tired of the interlopers in their midst. In 1760, they besieged the fort, massacred most of its surrendering garrison, and burned its wooden buildings to the ground.

Meanwhile, in 1748, intrepid Stephen Holston had followed the river that bears his name from its Virginia source to its confluence with the French Broad, and beyond; he was the first to travel the full length of the Tennessee River to the Ohio and the Mississippi. Holston's River charted a new course from Virginia to upper East Tennessee, and settlement spread out from it along the Watauga and the Nolichucky. Firstcomers found themselves so far removed from North Carolina's protection that, in 1772, they formed a local government of their own called the Watauga Association to maintain law and order on the western frontier.

This successful experiment in self-government produced a legendary leader, John Sevier. In 1780, he and Col. Isaac Shelby mustered the first volunteers from the future Volunteer State, and crossed from the Watauga Settlements into North Carolina to defeat the British at the Revolutionary War battle of King's Mountain.

In 1777, North Carolina's wartime government had acknowledged the Cherokees' claim to most of East Tennessee as their traditional hunting grounds: The Indian boundary was set just north of the future site of Greeneville. But four years later, the state of North Carolina announced that only the lands lying southwest of the French Broad River, and south of the Tennessee, were reserved to the Cherokee. All the rest of the state's territory beyond the mountains was offered for sale, cheap, to prospective homesteaders or investors. As a result, the portions of present-day Knox County north of the Holston and the Tennessee (as well as the land between the Holston and the French Broad) were up for grabs.

This statue of John Sevier represents the state of Tennessee in the Hall of Fame at the U.S. Capitol in Washington, D.C. Before becoming Tennessee's first governor, Sevier was governor of the lost state of Franklin; he also was elected to the United States Congress from two states, North Carolina and Tennessee. Meanwhile, his two wives (Sarah Hawkins and "Bonny Kate" Sherrill) had presented him with seventeen children. McClung Historical Collection

No sooner was the "Land Grab Act" passed than a party of explorers hastened across the mountains in search of desirable property. James White, Robert Love, Francis Alexander Ramsey, and others followed the French Broad through the Great Smokies to the Forks of the Rivers, and made their way down the north side of the Tennessee to an area they christened "Grassy Valley." They found, and purchased, ideal future homesites, but unexpected events forced them to put their moving plans on hold.

Early in 1784, North Carolina suddenly ceded all her land beyond the mountains to the United States government in settlement of Revolutionary War debts. Congress had recently enacted the Jeffersonian Ordinance encouraging the formation of new states in the west, so the overmountain settlers proceeded to organize one. They elected John Sevier governor of the "State of Franklin," selected Jonesborough as its capital, adopted a state constitution, and applied for admission to the Federal Union. Many of Knox County's future leaders proclaimed allegiance to the new state: Among its officials were James White, speaker of the senate; John Manefee, speaker of the house of representatives; and Francis Alexander Ramsey, secretary of the constitutional convention.

Meanwhile, North Carolina's legislators were having second thoughts. In November 1784, they repealed the Act of Cession. The Franklin government chose to ignore this fact, and for a time, East Tennessee had two governments, issuing contradictory orders.

In June 1785, Franklin's Governor Sevier met with a number of Cherokee chieftains at Dumplin Creek, and negotiated a treaty that permitted white settlement as far southwest as the ridge between the Little River and the Little Tennessee River. Relying on this agreement,

At the county's eastern edge, on Dave Smith Road, is a rare example of the cantilevered barns built by the area's earliest settlers. Metropolitan Planning Commission's Historic Buildings Survey

Howard Chandler Christy's huge painting, The Signing of the U.S. Constitution, hangs in the national Capitol in Washington, D.C. This detail shows William Blount standing beside the desk, next in line to affix his signature. President George Washington, at right, presided over this historic occasion. Three years later, he appointed Blount governor of the newly created Territory of the United States South of the River Ohio. Courtesy of Knoxville, Knox County Constitutional Bicentennial Commission

settlers began moving into every quadrant of what is now Knox County: east, at the Forks of the Rivers and along Flat Creek; north, on Beaver and Bull Run ridges; south, near the French Broad River and Little River; and west, in Hind's Valley and Grassy Valley.

But before the first forest-clearings could be made, the Indians had repudiated the Treaty of Dumplin Creek. Furthermore, the Cherokee Nation had gone over the heads of the disputing states by demanding—and getting—a meeting with representatives of the United States government. In November 1785, the resulting Treaty of Hopewell confirmed the earlier Indian boundary north of Greeneville. The federal government not only nullified Sevier's treaty with the Cherokee, but refused to admit the state of Franklin to the Union.

In 1788, John Sevier was arrested and taken under armed guard to Morganton, North Carolina, to be tried for treason on the grounds that he had set up a rival government within the territory of a sovereign state. Sevier's sons James and John, along with a group of friends that included future Knox Countians Jesse Greene and Dr. James Cozby, interrupted the trial and helped him to escape.

In 1789, like Sir Walter Raleigh's Lost Colony, the state of Franklin disappeared without a trace. John Sevier's arrest had convinced his adherents that separate statehood was a hopeless cause, and they responded by electing him to represent the Western District in the North Carolina Senate; he was a member of the North Carolina convention that ratified the United States Constitution, at long last. In 1790, he became one of North Carolina's first representatives in the United States Congress, but his term ended abruptly when the state conveyed her western lands to the federal government—again.

At the Holston Treaty Meeting, Governor William Blount's official party was alarmingly outnumbered by the Cherokees' forty-one chieftains and twelve hundred braves. This Is Tennessee, *by Mary U. Rothrock*

From The French Broad - Holston Country, *edited by Mary U. Rothrock*

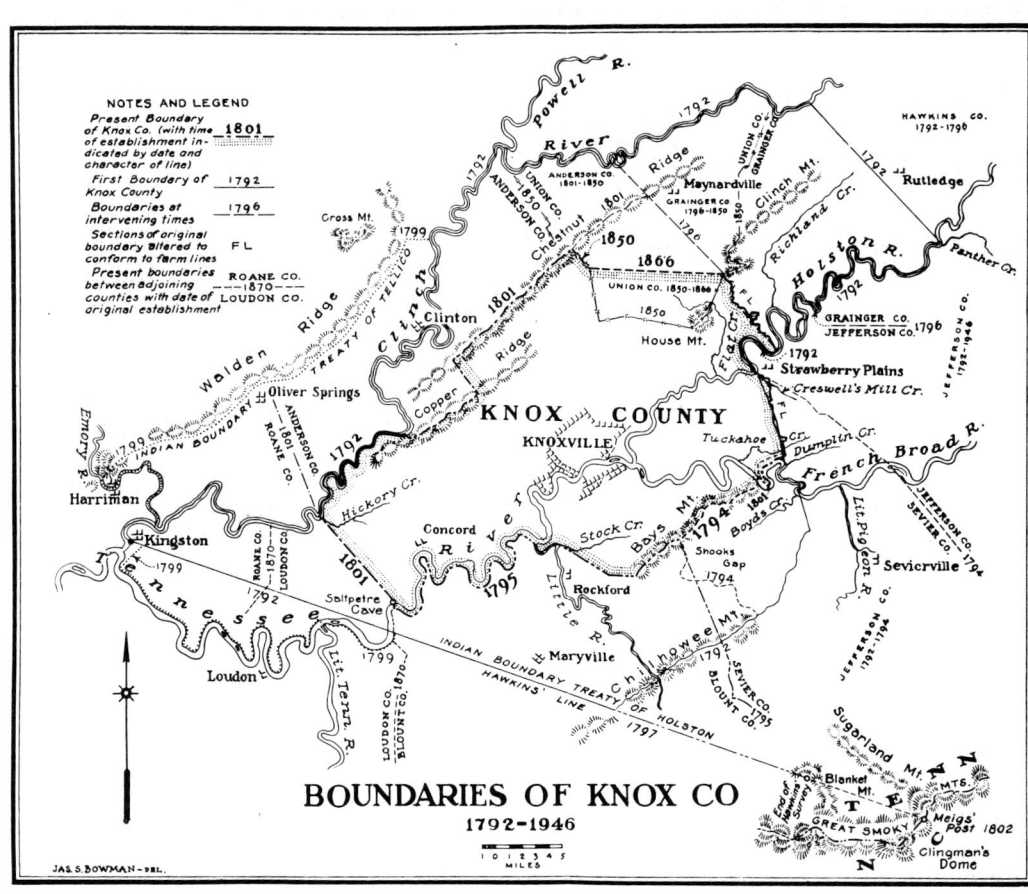

This time, the ceded area was immediately organized as the Territory of the United States South of the River Ohio, a title shortened in everyday usage to "The Southwest Territory." As its governor and superintendent of Indian affairs, President George Washington selected William Blount of North Carolina. After appointing civil and military officials for the territory's Washington District (in upper East Tennessee) and its Mero District (on the Cumberland), Blount wisely decided that concluding a new treaty with the Cherokee should take precedence over all other business.

In 1786, James White had built a two story log house near the spot where First Creek meets the Tennessee River, and had enlarged it with outbuildings and a protective stockade. Governor Blount chose White's Fort, which was only a day's journey away from the Indian towns on the Little Tennessee, as the site of his all-important confrontation with the Cherokee chiefs.

Knowing the Indians' love of pomp and pageantry, Blount appointed a master of ceremonies, Trooper James Armstrong, whose previous military service in European capitals qualified him as an expert on courtly etiquette and protocol. On the appointed day, the governor donned a uniform lavishly trimmed with gold lace, and received his guests in a bunting-draped pavilion erected at the mouth of First Creek. Not to be outdone, the chieftains were arrayed in all their finery, including gifts received at former treaty meetings. (One sachem had draped himself with yards of silver lace, and was carrying a crimson parasol!) With the forty-one chiefs came twelve hundred Cherokee braves who viewed the proceedings, like spectators in an amphitheatre, from the sloping sides of the First Creek valley.

After several days of alternate parlaying and feasting, the Treaty of Holston was signed on July 2, 1791. Governor Blount had managed to purchase the Cherokees' claim to all of present-day Knox County and its surrounding area, and he decided to establish the territory's seat of government at the site of the successful treaty meeting. James White agreed to sell enough land for the new capital, and White's son-in-law, Charles McClung, laid out a town containing sixty-four half-acre parcels that were assigned to purchasers by a public lottery on October 3, 1791.

Blount christened his capital city "Knoxville" in honor of Maj. Gen. Henry Knox, the secretary of war in President Washington's cabinet, and erected a handsome residence for his family with a one-room office building in its garden for the territorial capitol. There, on June 11, 1792, the governor signed an ordinance creating Knox County and naming Knoxville its county seat.

Two counties, Knox and Jefferson, were established on that day, but Knox, with an area of 1,260 square miles, was by far the larger. It once extended as far north as the forks of the Clinch and Powell rivers, east to the spot where Panther Creek flows into the Holston, south to the crest of Chilhowee Mountain, and west to the point where the Clinch River joins the Tennessee. It thus included parts of today's Anderson, Union, Grainger, Sevier, Blount, Loudon, and Roane counties; the future townsites of Oliver Springs, Oak Ridge, Clinton, Maynardville, Alcoa, Maryville, Lenoir City, Kingston, and Harriman were all within its boundaries. It also encompassed the eventual sites of TVA's Norris and Fort Loudoun dams.

So large an area was unwieldy. In pioneer days, an unofficial rule governing the size of counties required that any resident be able to ride horseback to the county seat and return home in a single day. So, as one after another adjacent county was created, Knox County was reduced by 1866 to its more manageable present size of 526 square miles.

From the beginning, the county's history was shaped by its four topographical divisions lying north, east, south, and west of the county seat. In the center, William Blount's "planned city" crowned an elevated rectangular plateau overlooking the broad Tennessee River. South of the river, row after row of forest-clad foothills marched toward the smoke-blue mountains. On the east, the placid Holston and the palisaded French Broad bestowed their alluvial riches. In the north, high parallel ridges enclosed glens alive with bubbling springs. Westward, the great, green Valley of East Tennessee fanned out into rolling meadowlands.

In every compass point, communities sprang up around the first fortified cabins that were called "stations," and incoming settlers made a profound discovery that is shared by natives and newcomers today: In spite of trials and tribulations, Knox County is a place that the heart calls home.

Knox County—where the lakes and mountains meet. Knoxville Convention and Visitors Bureau

East Knox County's most industrious early settler, the Reverend Samuel Carrick, was a farmer and a pedagogue, as well as a Presbyterian minister. He established Knox County's first church, Lebanon-in-the-Fork in 1791, and Knoxville's First Presbyterian Church in 1792; in 1794, he became the first president of Blount College, now The University of Tennessee. In 1792, he opened a classical seminary at his home on the Holston River, at the western end of present-day Boyds Bridge. Lloyd Branson's painting shows farmer Carrick interviewing his first student, Hugh Lawson White, who later married his teacher's daughter Elizabeth, at right. Courtesy of Nancy McMillan Rodgers

Chapter 1

East Knox County

Rivers were the interstate highways of pioneer days. Whether they followed the French Broad River from North Carolina or the Holston from Virginia, eighteenth century travellers approached what is now Knox County from the east, and it was in that area that the greatest concentration of early settlements took place.

When, in 1783, North Carolina offered all the state's western lands for sale, a party of explorers hastened across the mountains in search of desirable property. At this time James White, Francis A. Ramsey, and Alexander McMillan found their future homesites, but the ownership of their chosen land was in dispute: The Cherokee insisted that the 1777 treaty with the state of North Carolina, which set the Indian boundary just north of Greeneville, was still in effect.

While John Sevier was governor of the short-lived state of Franklin, he met with the Cherokee chiefs at Dumplin Creek in June of 1785, and obtained the rights to all of present day Knox County. This good news travelled fast, and by summer's end, the first settlers arrived in the Forks of the Rivers and along Flat Creek—only to find that the Cherokee had reneged on their agreement.

But the settlers had come to stay. Col. John Sawyers of Virginia built a sturdy fort east of Corryton, not far from where Little Flat Creek Baptist Church—the first of its denomination in Knox County—would be established in 1796. The McBees, Howells, Carters, Loves, and Cobbs took up land grants in the rich Flat Creek/Holston basin. Alexander McMillan located on the opposite side of the Holston, at Strawberry Plains, while Robert Armstrong, Jeremiah Jack, and Capt. Thomas Gillespie cleared fertile fields in the triangle between the rivers. Devereaux Gilliam built a log station at the very point where the two streams flowed together, and operated a ferry nearby on the Holston for the convenience of his neighbors. George McNutt's land was below the Forks, on the north side of the Tennessee River, near Robert Houston's residence at Cold Spring. And James White lingered on the French Broad (at Riverdale) for a year before moving downstream to his permanent home that was the nucleus of Knoxville.

These settlers were not only the first, but the most fortunate. Aside from a threatned raid on Captain Gillespie's station, and the theft of several horses from Flat Creek farms, the eastern area was mercifully spared the Indian attacks that terrorized the rest of Knox County.

East Knox County's prehistoric landmarks:

At the Forks of the Rivers, the Holston and the French Broad join to form the Tennessee. Photograph by Bill Tracy

House Mountain rises in splendid isolation from level farmland to an elevation of more than twenty-one hundred feet. It became a state park in 1987. This photograph appeared in The Scenic Resources of the Tennessee Valley, *published by TVA in 1938.*

The weathered inscription on this tombstone reads: "Elizabeth M. Carrick, consort of the Rev. S. Carrick. Died Sept. 1793."

Immediately after his wife's death, which occurred when a Cherokee and Creek war party was about to attack Knoxville, Samuel Carrick was summoned to militia duty. Women of the neighborhood brought Elizabeth's body down stream by dugout canoe for midnight burial in the churchyard of Lebanon-in-the-Fork. Photograph by Dan Yearout

The First Stone House in Knox County — Photo by Robert M. McBride

Francis Alexander Ramsey was one of the group of explorers who visited this area in 1783. At that time he purchased five hundred acres of land near the junction of the French Broad and Holston rivers and named the property "Swan Pond" for its small lake that was a nesting place for waterfowl. He did not return to take up residence until 1792. In 1796, he employed London-trained architect Thomas Hope to construct a "gentleman's manor" of rough-cut pink marble with a belt course, window tops, and quoins of blue limestone.

In 1952, under the leadership of Ellen McClung Berry, the Knox County Chapter of the Association for the Preservation of Tennessee Antiquities purchased Ramsey House, and opened it to the public as a period museum. Research and restoration are on-going: in the interest of historical accuracy, the small portico shown in Robert McBride's photograph has been removed.

Charming Margaret Russell was married in turn to James Cowan, Thomas Humes, and Francis Alexander Ramsey. She was widowed three times, and each time became the mother of a posthumous son! After Colonel Ramsey's death in 1820, she wisely declined to re-wed. This photograph of a daguerreotype was provided by the McClung Historical Collection of the Knox County Library.

Fine pink marble, first used as a building material in 1796 for Francis Alexander Ramsey's handsome home, is still quarried at nearby Asbury. Photograph by Bill Tracy

Dr. J. G. M. Ramsey was born in a log house on the Swan Pond property in 1797, and named for the Reverend James Gettys McGready, a Presbyterian evangelist his father much admired.

He built his home, "Mecklenburg," at the spot where the Holston and the French Broad rivers join to form the Tennessee, and there he wrote his Annals of Tennessee to the End of the 18th Century, *the definitive early history of this area. The notes and manuscript for a second volume of Tennessee history were destroyed when Mecklenburg was burned by Union soldiers in 1863. The disfiguring railroad bridge built across the Forks of the Rivers in the 1870s, to transport marble from East Knox County quarries, passed directly over the ruins of Mecklenburg. From a portrait by Lloyd Branson*

In the 1790s, the narrow trail to Greeneville, Jonesborough, and Virginia (US 11E) was widened to a wagon road, and McBee's Ferry began transporting goods and travelers across the Holston River. Strawberry Plains Pike was Knox County's link with the eastern seaboard when "Wooddale" was built beside it in 1800. *Historic Buildings Survey, conducted by the Metropolitan Planning Commission*

"Trafalgar," designed by Thomas Hope, was the home of John Kain whose daughters, Mattie and Kittie, were among the nation's first five coeds at Blount College in 1804. The unique herringbone-brick mansion, completed in 1807 at Kain's Bend on the Holston River, was demolished to make way for the Southern Railway's John Sevier Yards. The graves of John and Mary (McMullen) Kain are within the enclosure. *UTK Special Collections Library*

The Legg/England house on Rutledge Pike was built as a stagecoach inn in the 1830s after the completion of a second road to Virginia via Rutledge and Kingsport (US 11W). James K. Polk spent the night here in 1845, on the way to Washington for his inauguration as president of the United States. MPC Survey

Dr. George W. Arnold followed this route when he came from Roanoke, Virginia, to Knox County in 1838. "Chesterfield," the house he built on Old Rutledge Pike, has since been owned and cherished by five generations of the Nicely family. Photograph by Ron Childress, from Knoxville: Fifty Landmarks

Knox County has everything, including a mining town!

In the 1920s, clouds of white dust from the American Zinc smelting plant hovered over the commissary, dormitories, and rows of company houses at Mascot, where zinc mining began in 1906. Courtesy of Katie Morell Dalton

This photograph, from the American Zinc, Lead, and Smelting Company's Collection, shows the recreation center provided for black employees living at Mascot in the 1920s.

East of the Magnolia Avenue Viaduct is the area christened Cold Spring Farm by its original owner, Robert Houston, the first sheriff of Knox County. According to tradition, it was he who built the handsome brick house that was enlarged and modernized early in this century as a haven "for destitute women of good character over sixty years old." Mount Rest Home is still in operation at 2639 McCalla Avenue. Knoxville Journal, *1967*

In a mere twenty years, the frontier outpost of James White's Fort turned into the bustling capital of the state of Tennessee, and James White moved to his farm east of First Creek in search of peace and quiet. In 1900, Bonny Kate Chapter of the DAR placed this marker at the site of his two-story log farmhouse on Riverside Drive.

Adaptive use has done wonders for the house in the background, which was built by Knox County Sheriff Samuel McCammon in 1842. Now the headquarters of a plumbing company, it was mercifully missed by the access ramp of the new South Knoxville Bridge. Knoxville News-Sentinel

A slip of the chisel?

This circa 1907 postcard-photograph shows the DAR marker's original identification of Knoxville's founder as Rev. James White. The inscription was changed to read Gen. James White, as seen above. Author's Collection

James White gave a portion of his farm to his daughter Melinda, the wife of Col. John Williams who fought in the War of 1812 and the Creek War, was U.S. Minister to Guatemala under President John Quincy Adams, and represented Tennessee in the United States Senate from 1815 to 1823.

A twentieth century descendant, Thomas Lanier Williams, changed his first name to emphasize his heritage: as "Tennessee" Williams, he became a famous playwright.

Tradition holds that while Colonel Williams was absent during the Creek War, Melinda White Williams had this house built as a surprise for him. "Travelers Rest" in Nashville is almost an exact duplicate; its chatelaine, Mrs. John Overton, was James White's daughter, Mary.

Photograph by Ernest B. Robertson, Jr., 1958

James Mason became Knoxville's first Negro taxpayer in 1866, when he bought a house and lot on West Cumberland Avenue. In 1879, he opened a school in his home for black children who could neither hear nor speak. In 1881, he transferred his ten pupils to the Williams house, which had been purchased by the state for a Negro branch of the Tennessee School for the Deaf. The Williams property, at 2325 Dandridge Avenue, is now the Sertoma Learning Center. Beck Cultural Exchange Center

Andrew Jackson came to Knoxville so often that a room was always kept ready for him at the home of his friend, James Kennedy, Sr., on East Church Street. After Jackson's death in 1845, the ladies of the Kennedy family mounted his watercolor portrait against a background of his favorite quilt. The "memento," in its original frame, is in the collection of Blount Mansion Association. Photograph by Nick Myers

The home of William G. Brownlow—Methodist minister, newspaper editor, Unionist leader, governor of Tennessee, and United States Senator—was on East Cumberland Avenue. Parson Brownlow entertained many famous guests here, and long after his death in 1877, notable visitors to Knoxville paid courtesy calls upon his widow. A brass plaque on the hall-tree from this house lists six presidents of the United States—Andrew Johnson, Ulysses S. Grant, Rutherford B. Hayes, William McKinley, Theodore Roosevelt, and William Howard Taft—who hung their hats there. UTK Special Collections Library

This marble monument, in the Confederate Cemetery at 1715 Bethel Avenue, was erected in 1892 by the Ladies' Memorial Associaiton of Knoxville to honor the more than sixteen hundred CSA soldiers buried there. Directory of Civil War Monuments and Memorials in Tennessee, *1963*

In 1895, Rabbi Isaac Winick became the first resident rabbi of Heska Amuna Synagogue at the corner of Vine and Temperance streets, where this group picture of the religious school was made in 1901. Fifth from the left in the front row is the rabbi's son, Ben, whose daughter, Barbara Winick Bernstein, kindly provided the photograph.

Heska Amuna Synagogue on Kingston Pike was built in 1961.

Knox County's first electric streetcar line was formally opened on May 1, 1890, when a procession of trolley cars carried leading citizens to Lake Ottosee, formerly known as Beaman's Lake. Greater Knoxville Chamber of Commerce

The host on that occasion was the president of the Knoxville Electric Street Railway Company, William Gibbs McAdoo, Jr., a descendant of Knox County pioneers. After a long and bitter struggle, McAdoo lost control of Knoxville's streetcar system in 1897, but that was by no means the end of his career. In 1913, he became secretary of the treasury, and is seated on the left of President Woodrow Wilson in this photograph of the cabinet, from his autobiography, Crowded Years. *In 1914, he was married in the White House, to the president's daughter, Eleanor Wilson.*

Before its present building was erected on the site, Catholic High School occupied the former residence of the Branner family, who gave a 100-foot right-of-way through their extensive property for access to Lake Ottosee. Knoxville Mayor H. Bryan Branner named the wide street Magnolia Avenue in honor of his mother, Mrs. George M. Branner, nee Magnolia Bryan. McClung Historical Collection

In the 1890s, the convenient streetcars made Lake Ottosee Knox County's favorite recreation area. In addition to rental rowboats, it offered a sandy "wading-beach" and a shallow cove for swimming, enclosed for safety with a "boardwalk."

After the turn of the century, when a "Midway" opened on its shores, Lake Ottosee was renamed Chilhowee Park. The amusement area featured a roller coaster, and a splendid merry-go-round with a calliope; they remained in use until the 1940s. UTK Special Collections Library

Not to be outdone by Fountain City, Chilhowee Park boasted a mineral spring surrounded by picnic tables. Author's Collection

Conservation, *a word coined early in this century to mean "the wise use of natural resources," was the theme of three successive (and successful) expositions sponsored by Knox County's business community at Chilhowee Park. This rustic bridge and the buildings behind it were constructed for the first Appalachian Exposition in 1910. Author's Collection*

A pioneer log cabin was the equivalent of today's mobile home. With considerable effort, it could be moved to a new location.

The modest West Knox County birthplace of Adm. David Farragut was dismantled in 1910 and reassembled on the Appalachian Exposition grounds, where it later burned. Author's Collection

The last stop on the streetcar line was Burlington, where Cal Johnson's racetrack is now a city street called Speedway Circle.
Phil Parmalee exhibited Knox County's first airplane there during the Appalachian Exposition in 1910, and spectators gladly paid the munificent sum of fifty cents to see the plane take off, circle the track once, and land again. Stables for Cal Johnson's thoroughbred racehorses appear in the background of Fayette VanDeventer's snapshot. Beck Cultural Exchange Center

The 1910 Appalachian Exposition was such a boon to business that it was repeated the following year. House Hasson Hardware Company's 1911 business envelopes advertised the many attractions of the enlarged and expanded coming event. Author's Collection

At the Appalachian Exposition in 1911, an enterprising photographer provided his customers with "props," and posed them against a painted backdrop in this pennant-plastered touring car. The "FHS" banner probably represented Farragut High School, the first in Knox County. UTK Special Collections Library

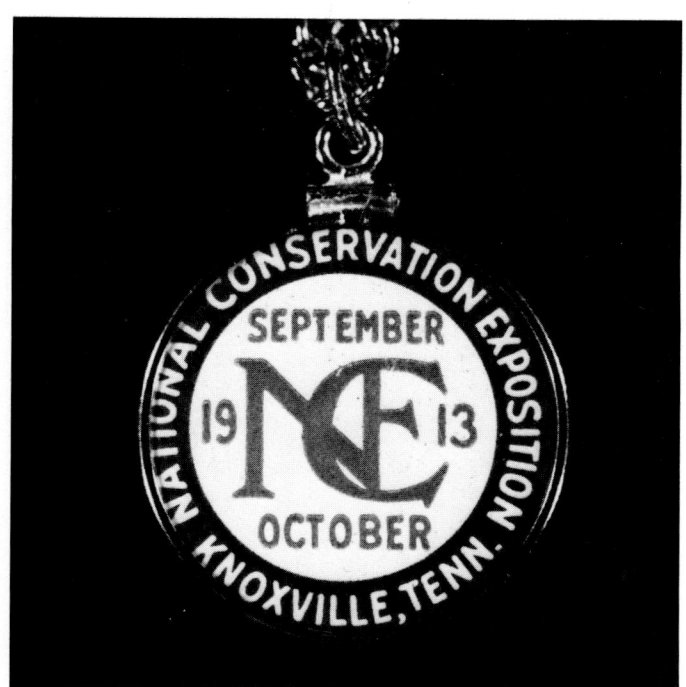

Author's Collection

Having hosted two outstanding regional events, Chilhowee Park was promoted to the national level in 1913. The following photographs (from a weighty tome entitled *The First Exhibition of Conservation and Its Builders*) attest to the remarkable scope of that ambitious undertaking.

One of the imposing exhibition halls built in 1913 to replace the rustic structures of the earlier Appalachian Expositions was the Machinery and Liberal Arts Building, with eighty-thousand square feet of floor space. It overlooked the lake from the present site of the Jacobs Building.

This unusual building, representing the mining interests of Tennessee and Kentucky, was faced with large chunks of iridescent black coal.

At night the exposition grounds were ablaze with electric light. Here, the East Tennessee Building is "outlined with incandescent globes."

Banquets for visiting dignitaries were held on a gaily decorated houseboat moored beside the lake.

Booker T. Washington was the guest of the Exposition on October 20, and a parade through the grounds ended at the bandstand where he spoke. In this photograph by Knoxville's outstanding black photographer, Boyd Browder, the first car shown skirting the midway carried members of the still-active Acacia Rose Circle, founded in 1902. Margaret Singleton Carson, the little girl in the picture, kindly provided this information. Beck Cultural Exchange Center

Although they number less than 10 percent of the county's total population (28,006 of 319,694 in 1980), black citizens have an integral place in Knox County's history. The official report of the First National Conservation Exposition records that this building for the Negro department "was designed by a Negro architect, built by a Negro contractor and Negro workmen, with money subscribed by Negro citizens of Knoxville."

One by one, the imposing exhibition halls were destroyed by fire. Today, the sole survivor is the bandstand given by Knox County's marble producers to the Appalachian Exposition of 1910. Its restoration in 1976 was a major project of the Greater Knoxville American Revolution Bicentennial Commission.

But each September, Chilhowee Park reenacts the early expositions by hosting the ever-popular Tennessee Valley Fair.

The Marble Band Stand, Appalachian Exposition, Knoxville, Tenn.

Akima Club brought an outstanding year-round attraction to Chilhowee park in 1966: the region's first planetarium, featured at the Students' Museum. Students' Museum, Inc.

The Knoxville Zoo, once a small menagerie in Chilhowee Park whose most impressive inmate was a talking crow, now occupies a model 100-acre zoological park where the most popular attraction is Little Diamond, the first African elephant born in the Western Hemisphere. Knoxville Convention and Visitors Bureau

When the growing zoo needed to expand outside Chilhowee Park, it annexed a large level area beside I-40. This reclaimed land was once the city's Cherry Street Dump!
From the simulated African Plains to the solar-heated reptile house, this outstanding zoo's thousands of denizens live happily in environmental enclosures designed for their comfort, and for their visitors' enjoyment. Appalachian Zoological Society

East of Chilhowee Park and Burlington, a new subdivision was developed in a scenic area overlooking the Holston River and the distant mountains.

This golfer's view of Holston Hills Country Club was taken in 1927, while the challenging course was still under construction. McClung Historical Collection

When the second of Knoxville's annual Dogwood Trails opened in Holston Hills in 1957, motorists looked for guidance to green arrows nailed on telephone poles and trees. Since 1960, all six trails have been marked with easy-to-follow pink dots painted on the pavement of the chosen streets. Dogwood Arts Festival

Knox County's oldest business, Howell Nurseries, has been in continuous operation at the same location since 1786! Azaleas were first introduced here by this nursery, and long before there were Dogwood Trails, sightseers drove out to Boyd's Bridge Pike at Easter time to admire the fields of rainbow-colored blooms. The McClung Historical Collection contains this photograph of Howell Nurseries' exhibit at the 1956 Home Show.

Still to be seen on Dandridge Avenue is the Mabry-Hazen House, where Confederate and Union officers were billeted in turn during the Civil War. It was the home of Joseph A. Mabry, Jr. who, along with his brother-in-law William G. Swan, had given Market Square to the city of Knoxville in 1853. As a result of a bitter business feud General Mabry, his son Joseph A. Mabry III, and Thomas O'Conner were all killed on October 18, 1882, in an exchange of pistol shots on Gay Street. Photograph by Ron Childress for Knoxville: Fifty Landmarks

That strange object rising from the crest of Mabry's Hill is the city watertower with its attendant standpipe, in use from 1882 until the 1920s. McClung Historical Collection

This steam-powered intake station on Riverside Drive pumped untreated water up to the hilltop tower which distributed it through the city's mains by gravity flow. Author's Collection

In the late nineteenth and early twentieth centuries, the wooded slopes of Mabry's Hill were filled with homes and businesses of the black community.

Sylvester McBee's popular fruitstand was on East Vine Street, near the Odd Fellows Hall. Beck Cultural Exchange Center

This mule-drawn surrey with a dignified passenger is parked in front of the Carnegie Library at Vine and Nelson streets.

A marble plaque on the 1918 building read: "... erected by the city commissioners of Knoxville in recognition of the faithful efforts of Charles W. Cansler, who first conceived the idea of this library for his race—and who aided materially in securing it." Beck Cultural Exchange Center

In the days before air conditioning, paper fans were often furnished to churches by neighborhood businessmen. This one advertised the Wheeler Mortuary on East Vine Street, and portrayed the 1936 wedding party of Mr. and Mrs. A. R. Wheeler. Author's Collection

Joseph Delaney, one of the nation's outstanding black artists, came home to Knox County in 1987 as artist-in-residence at The University of Tennessee, Knoxville. He is famous for his paintings of parades, and street scenes like this rousing welcome to the Al G. Field Minstrels, dated 1948 and titled "Vine and Central." UT Center for Educational Video and Photography

Austin-East High School's jazz band won the world championship at the 1975 International Jazz Festival in Jamaica. 1976 A-E Roadrunner

Born in slavery in 1844, Calvin F. Johnson became one of Knox County's wealthiest citizens. In addition to a racetrack in Burlington, he owned a number of downtown business properties, including the Cal Johnson Building at Vine and Central. *McClung Historical Collection*

Cal Johnson, who had been Knoxville's first black city alderman in 1883, posed in 1922 beside the fountain he presented to Cal Johnson City Park. Highway construction and urban renewal destroyed all but a small remnant of the tree-shaded recreation area that once bordered the east side of First Creek between Vine and Cumberland Avenues. *Beck Cultural Exchange Center*

After World War II, when "Urban Renewal" was touted as a sure cure for the sociological and financial ills of American cities, the homes and businesses of black East Knoxville were leveled to the ground, streets were rerouted, and the contours of the hills rearranged into a vast expanse of raw, red clay. The first redevelopment occurred in 1960, when the $5 million Civic Auditorium/Coliseum was completed. *Greater Knoxville Chamber of Commerce*

The Auditorium side of the multi-purpose structure provided comfortable seating for plays, and for performances of the 100-member Knoxville Symphony Orchestra, under the direction of its composer/conductor, David VanVactor. *Greater Knoxville Chamber of Commerce*

The larger Coliseum could convert with ease from ice shows to formal Dogwood Balls, or from circuses to big-name concerts. Knoxville Convention and Visitors Bureau

After standing for more than half a century on Woodlawn Pike, James White's house was purchased by the City Association of Women's Clubs, and reassembled in 1970 near the James White Memorial Auditorium/Coliseum, on the opposite side of the First Creek valley from its original location. Because the chosen site in the Mountain View Urban Renewal Area had been slated for commercial development, it took an act of Congress to free it for historical purposes! This Knoxville News-Sentinel *photograph shows the house and the reconstructed out-buildings of White's Fort in various stages of completion.*

Whatever happened to First Creek? It went underground during the 1960s when, in preparation for the coming of the interstate highways, level space for a downtown loop was created by encasing the creek in a gigantic concrete culvert. Author's Collection

By 1975, the Mountain View Urban Renewal Area had not only acquired public parking facilities and the Public Safety Building, but also the ultra-modern Hyatt-Regency Hotel with glass elevators that emerged through the roof to command a view of the city. Photo by Bill Tracy

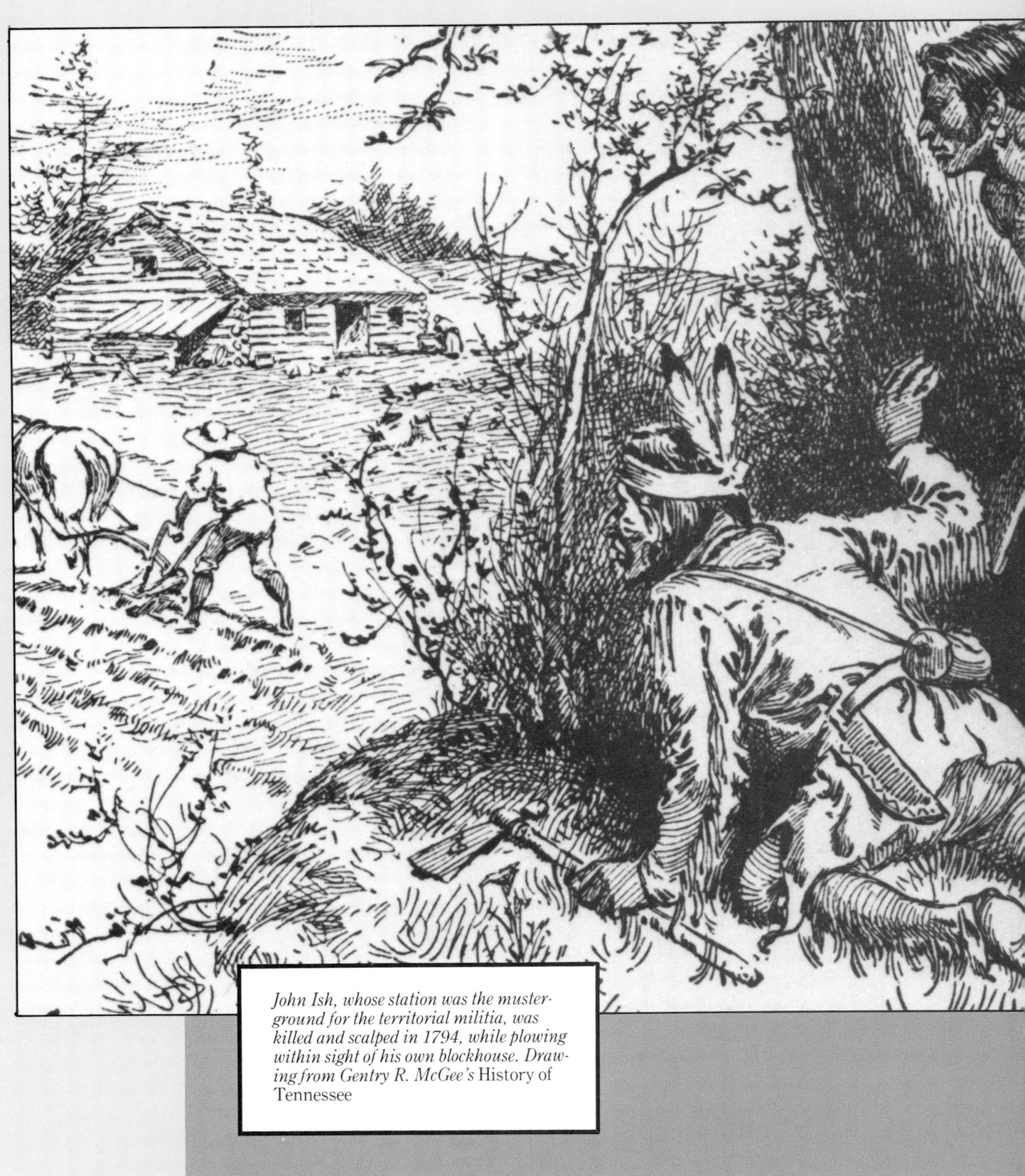

John Ish, whose station was the muster-ground for the territorial militia, was killed and scalped in 1794, while plowing within sight of his own blockhouse. Drawing from Gentry R. McGee's History of Tennessee

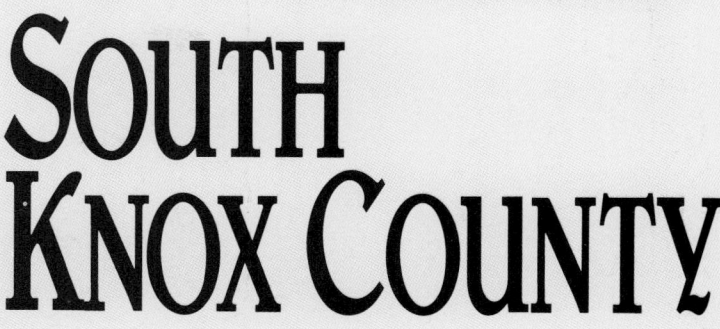

South Knox County

All of Knox County was once a part of the Lost State of Franklin, which existed from 1784 to 1790. Previously, the Cherokee had refused to part with their lands lying south of the Tennessee River, where the famous Warriors' Path to Virginia began at the Indian towns on the Little Tennessee. However, in 1785, when Franklin's governor, John Sevier, held a treaty meeting with the Cherokee chieftains at Dumplin Creek, a new boundary was set at the watershed between Little River and the Little Tennessee.

Although the Treaty of Dumplin Creek was promptly rescinded by the Cherokee, a few fearless pioneers proceded to move into what would become South Knox County. In fact, John Ish defiantly built a large blockhouse and a mill west of Little River, just within the disputed boundary line. (Its site was in Knox County until 1795, when Blount County was created.) Greene's Station, later known as Manifold's, stood on the southwest side of the French Broad River, where Jesse Greene's nearest neighbors were Dr. James Cozby and Jacob Kimberlin.

A series of Indian raids resulted when the state of Franklin attempted to force the Cherokee to abide by the treaty, and the Franklin militia angrily retaliated. As a result, the worst Indian massacre in Knox County's history took place in 1788 when twenty-eight persons—most of them women and children—were killed in an assault on Capt. William Gillespie's station at the mouth of Little River.

Gov. William Blount repurchased the southside area in 1791 at the Holston Treaty Meeting, and a straight line on the map from the western tip of Chilhowee Mountain to Southwest Point (Kingston) was the new Cherokee Boundary. Nevertheless, the Indian raids continued and John Sevier, who had been appointed brigadier general of the territorial militia, made Ish's Station his headquarters whenever troops were called out to protect the settlers.

In April of 1974, twenty Indians attacked the isolated cabin of William Casteel, scalping and mutilating all seven members of the family. Miraculously, ten year old Elizabeth Casteel survived, and was nursed back to health in the home of a neighbor, Dr. James Cozby. She later married into the Dunlap family, and lived to a ripe old age in the Kimberlin Heights Community!

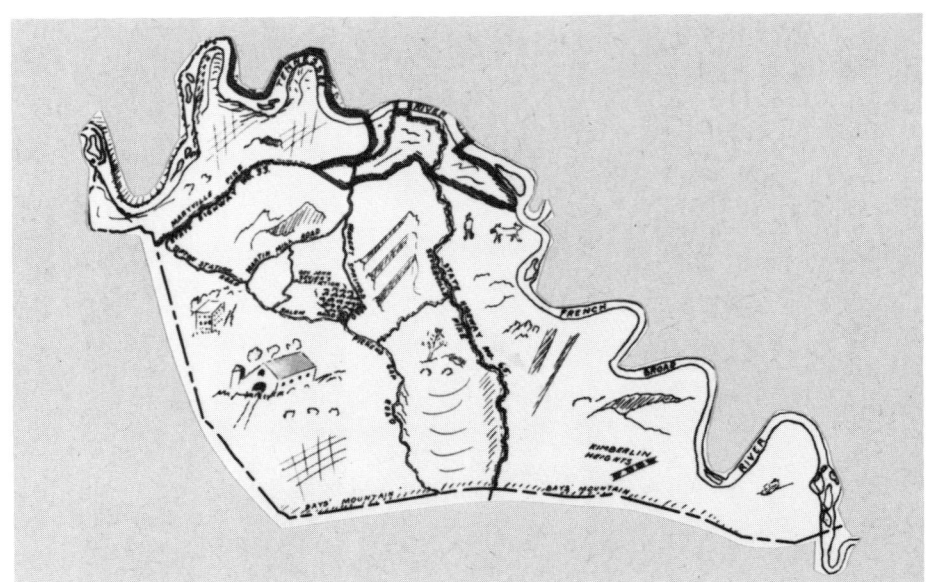

John Ish's nearest neighbors lived in the Stock Creek area, where the log wing of the Flanagan/Goddard Place on Goddard Road was built in 1790. Metropolitan Planning Commission's Historic Buildings Survey

A short stretch near the mouth of Little River became Knox County's southwestern boundary in 1795, when Blount County was created. Scenic Resources of the Tennessee Valley

John Sevier had made his headquarters south of the river, at Ish's Station, while serving as major general of the territorial militia. When he took up his duties as Tennessee's first governor in 1796, he elected to live in South Knox County, near his good friends Jesse Greene and Dr. James Cozby. His "Marble Springs Plantation," consisting of this main house and several outbuildings, is a Tennessee state shrine. *Knoxville Convention and Visitors Bureau*

"John Sevier" and friends, photographed by Hugh Lunsford at Marble Springs on opening day of the 1975 Dogwood Arts Festival. Left to right: Hal Stephens, a Sevier family member, in the uniform of a militia major general; Don Rapp, dressed as a militiaman; and James Robert Smith, in typical frontier garb. *Courtesy of Anne Lee Smith*

Early settlement was concentrated along the highways and by-ways of rivers and creeks. This house was a year old when Bishop Francis Asbury organized Knox County's first Methodist church in 1802 at Seven Islands on the French Broad River. MPC Survey

Since 1830, "Maple Bend" on Topside road has been a landmark at the mouth of Little River. MPC Survey

Cherokee Indians made the first riverboats. From them, white settlers learned how to hollow giant logs by burning and chipping into dugout canoes like this one in the Frank H. McClung Museum on the UT campus, which is 32½ feet long, 25 inches wide, and 10 inches deep. Photograph by Nick Myers

On the original Great Seal of the state of Tennessee, designed by Charles McClung in 1796, "Commerce" is represented by a river flatboat. Courtesy of Main Street Knoxville, Inc.

Knox County's official flag, designed by Mimi Kenan Smith in 1976, echoes the agriculture and commerce symbols of the original State Seal, but does not include the name of the sixteenth state because the county was four years old in 1796, when Tennessee came into being. Author's Collection

The trouble with flatboats was that they could only travel downstream with the current. But since 1827, when the paddle-wheeler Atlas *made it all the way from Mussel Shoals under its own steam, commercial traffic on the Tennessee River has moved upstream as well as down.* Scenic Resources of the Tennessee Valley

Following the arrival of the first passenger steamship (appropriately named the Knoxville*) in 1831, pleasure trips were popular on the Holston and the French Broad rivers, as well as on the Tennessee, until the century's end. The* River Queen, *which brought "excursion boating" back to Knox County in 1985, was succeeded in 1988 by the paddlewheeler* Robert E. Lee. Knoxville Convention and Visitors Bureau

By the mid-nineteenth century, most of the river's southside area was served by main and secondary roads. Knox County's sole example of Greek revival architecture was built in 1850, on Old Sevierville Pike. MPC Survey

Because the Keener-Hunt house on Woodlawn Road retains all of its original 1850 outbuildings, it won a Knoxville Heritage award for continuous historic preservation. MPC Survey

Fort Dickerson, built by the Union Army in 1863, was abandoned at the end of the Civil War, and forgotten—except by generations of South Knoxville boys. After Charles Wayland, who had played there, focussed attention on the fort in the 1950s, it became a city park. Hugh Lunsford made this photograph for the Knoxville Journal *in 1963, when the Battle of Fort Sanders was reenacted at Fort Dickerson. The battle's actual site was unavailable because it was occupied by Fort Sanders Hospital.*

Union earthworks forts, south of the river, were connected to the city by a pontoon bridge, and to protect the bridge from ramming by Confederate fireboats, a great iron chain was stretched from bank to bank, just above it. The chain served an even more important function by catching the food-laden rafts floated downstream by Unionist farmers living along the French Broad and the Holston rivers.

During the Civil War Centennial in 1963, this enormous anchor and a section of the great chain were unearthed by dredging operations near the south end of the Gay Street Bridge. The display was photographed at Confederate Memorial Hall. Courtesy of Jack Kirkland

From Longstreet's Heights, Confederate artillery bombarded the university in 1863. Early in the 1890s, a steel cable was stretched across the river, and passengers in the cable car ascended some three hundred feet from the mouth of Third Creek to the top of the dizzying heights. Cable service ended abruptly on February 18, 1894, when the cable snapped near the top of the incline, killing one passenger and leaving six others suspended over the river for several hours.

Now known as Cherokee Bluffs, this overlook is occupied by a condominium complex. During its construction, much of the jagged rock outcrop tumbled into Fort Loudon Lake. UTK Special Collections Library

In the 1870s, Col. Perez Dickinson raised bumper crops and blue-ribbon cattle on his riverside farm that included a large off-shore island, and curious crowds flocked to see Knox County's first mechanical reaper in operation. UTK Special Collections Library

Col. Perez Dickinson and guests, strolling through the grounds of "Island Home" on a balmy day in the 1870s. the colonel's Swiss gardener stands ready, at right, to answer questions and receive compliments on the knot-garden.

Island Home is now the superintendent's residence of the Tennessee School for the Deaf. History of Homes and Gardens of Tennessee

Until the 1920s, these pillars marked the entrance to Island Home, and this sign (composed by Col. Perez Dickinson himself) stood at the spot where the carriage drive divided:

> Welcome to view the beauties of this place
> Raised by the gardener's skill on Nature's face,
> But no rude hand should fruit or flower pull.
> For pulling fruit without the Gardener's leave,
> Mankind was ruined by our Mother Eve.

UT Center for Educational Video and Photography

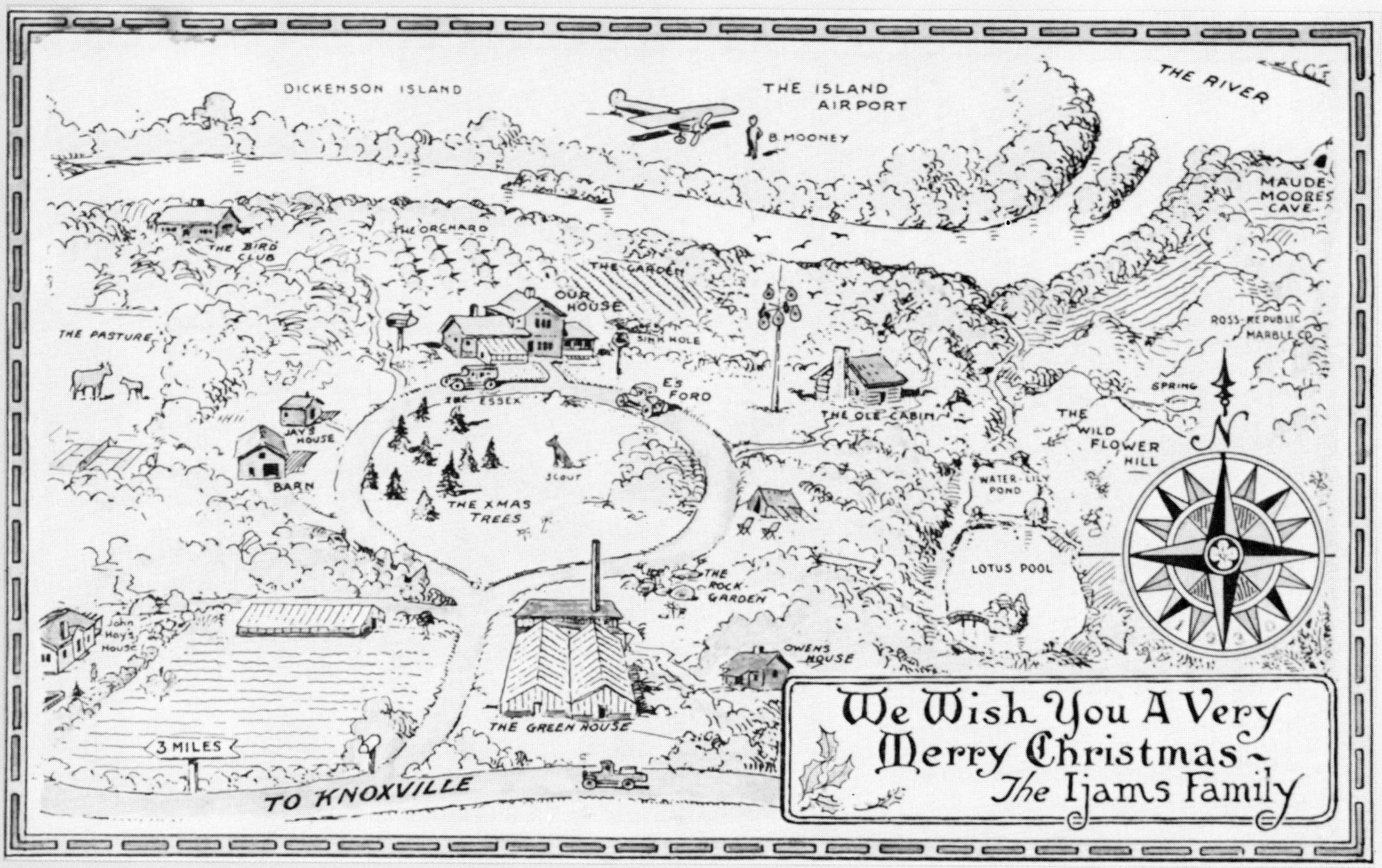

Harry P. Ijams' delightful map shows how the inshore acreage of Perez Dickinson's Island Home had been tranformed by 1930 into a wild bird sanctuary and a garden spot. Courtesy of Betty Jean Hay McNair, the little girl on the lawn of "John Hay's House."

Each holiday season, a Christmas tree is decorated for the birds at Ijams-Audubon Nature Center on Island Home Avenue. In the background of this 1982 Knoxville News-Sentinel *photo is the former home of Mr. and Mrs. Harry P. Ijams, whose riverside property became a very special park.*

Dickinson's Island was first used as a landing field in 1912, when the grand prize in a Knoxville Journal *contest was a short flight in an airplane built by the Wright Brothers. It became Island Airport for private planes and charter flights in 1930. Photograph by Bill Tracy*

The Tennessee River has been both a barrier and a gateway to South Knox County. Before there were bridges, there were ferry boats. The ferry at the Forks of the Rivers was the first in Knox County—and the last. McClung Historical Collection

In 1836, the operator of Hodges Ferry built a "noggin house," with an infill of field stone rubble between its outer and inner frame walls—the early-day equivalent of rock wool insulation. A subsequent owner brought the property up-to-date in the 1890s with a wraparound porch and Eastlake woodwork, and topped the project off by adding a transom and sidelights of ruby glass to the front door. MPC Survey

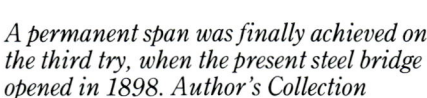

The sturdy stone piers erected by Knox County in the 1870s supported two wooden Gay Street bridges. The first, a "box bridge" with high weatherboarded sides, was blown off its underpinnings by a sudden gust of wind. The second was this privately-owned toll bridge that sagged in the middle, in use from 1880 to 1895. Its sign reads, "$5 FINE TO RIDE OR DRIVE FASTER THAN A WALK ON THIS BRIDGE." McClung Historical Collection

A permanent span was finally achieved on the third try, when the present steel bridge opened in 1898. Author's Collection

By the turn of the century, a thriving community had grown up around the Vestal Lumber Company, where logs arrived daily from Sevierville on the Smoky Mountain Railway. Commercial History of Tennessee

The Smoky Mountain Railroad's logging trains carried no passengers, but the Knoxville-to-Sevierville fast mail coach had room for people as well as packages and letters. It was a familiar sight on Old Sevierville Pike and was known to South Knox Countians as "the Omnibuggy." McClung Historical Collection

Dr. Ashley Sidney Johnson moved his correspondence Bible college from South Carolina to Knox County in 1887, when he purchased the property on which his great-grandfather, Jacob Kimberlin, found valuable lead deposits in 1787.

Flourishing Johnson Bible College was called "The School of the Evangelists" in 1893, when it opened in this chapel building that overlooks the campus from the apex of Kimberlin Heights. MPC Survey

The last vestige of Knox County's many "health resorts" is this gazebo on Neubert Springs Road, with its unique lattice-work of twisted tree-roots. It adorned the lawn of the Neubert Sulphur Springs Hotel, a popular turn-of-the-century watering spot. MPC Survey

This photograph of William H. Hastie, a native of South Knox County, appeared in the Knoxville Journal *on May 19, 1946, when he was appointed governor of the Virgin Islands. He became the first black federal district judge in 1949, and the first black justice of a U.S. Court of Appeals in 1968.*

The birthplace of Judge William H. Hastie was on Woodlawn Pike at Moody Avenue. Beck Cultural Exchange Center

There were two memorable events in the life of Isaiah Ford, a Knoxville printer. The first occurred early in his childhood, when he shook the hand of President Abraham Lincoln. The second took place in 1906, when he saved Knoxville's oldest house from being razed along with the State Street residence to which it was attached.

Isaiah Ford purchased and dismantled the log structure, numbering each hand-hewn timber as it was removed, and transported it across the river to Woodlawn Pike where the logs were reassembled. For fifty years, the house built by James White in 1786 was the home of the Ford family. UTK Special Collections Library

During the Prohibition Era, it was often said of South Knox County: "There are moonshine stills in them thar hills!" Author's Collection

Everyone who enjoys the mountains owes a debt of gratitude to these Knox countians whose photographs appeared in the golden anniversary publication of the Great Smoky Mountains National Park.

Mrs. W. P. Davis, Knox County's first woman representative in the Tennessee legislature, introduced in 1925 a bill to provide the first state funds to purchase available mountain land for a national park.

Col. David Chapman (who lived on Topside Road) headed the group of park-promoters that persuaded the city of Knoxville to contribute one third of the $500,000 asking price; he served as chairman and purchasing agent of the Great Smoky Mountains National Park Association. In 1929, Tennessee's General Assembly named the new state road to the new national park "Chapman Highway."

The entrance to the Great Smoky Mountains National Park for which the very first public appropriation was a gift of $167,000 from the city of Knoxville! Author's Collection

Early in the 1930s, the Scenic Loop Road to the Smokies was completed—from South Knox County through Sevierville, Gatlinburg, Townsend, and Maryville, back to South Knox County. Carlos Campbell's photograph shows Sunday tourists awed by this roadside view of The Chimneys.

Knox Countians took a proprietary delight in the park they had worked hard to obtain, and discovered a natural swimming pool at the base of Abrams Falls. Wylie Bowmaster took this picture there, in 1935.

"One picture is worth a thousand words."
Author's Collection

On September 4, 1940, President Franklin D. Roosevelt was helped from the platform of his private car at the Southern Railway Station. He was on his way to Newfound Gap, via Chapman Highway, for the official dedication of the Great Smoky Mountains National Park.
McClung Historical Collection

In 1967, April's canopy of white blossoms overarched West Redbud Drive, near the entrance to the Chapman Highway Dogwood Trail, which crosses the busy highway with a traffic light and continues on the other side. Knoxville's first Fall Color Trail opened here in October of 1987. Knoxville News-Sentinel

In 1914, the Knox County Court purchased 569 acres on the south side of the river for an agricultural experiment station to be administered by the University of Tennessee. Much of the land was reserved for dairying, which was the county's principal livestock enterprise. UT Center for Educational Video and Photography

The only access to the new southside farm was provided by Cherokee Bridge from Kingston Pike. The entrance to the narrow wooden bridge was across from the Alexander Bonnyman residence, which is now the Teen Center. UT Magazine, *Historical Edition*

When this early 1920s photograph was made, the peninsula enclosed by the river's horseshoe bend was "the Peter Blow place," a richly productive farm with a large white manor house on its highest hill. The family's private ferry to West Knoxville operated from a landing at the foot of Blow's Ferry Road. Author's Collection

For a century and a quarter, beautiful ante-bellum "Speedwell" stood near New Tazewell, Tennessee. In the 1950s, it was transported to Knox County by Dr. Frank T. Rogers. Its thousands of rosy bricks were numbered as they were removed, and re-laid on the site of the Peter Blow house. In 1988, Speedwell ceased to be a house museum, and is once again a private residence. Dogwood Arts Festival

There was great rejoicing when this new Alcoa Highway Bridge opened in the 1930s. It linked the two sections of the UT farm on its way to McGhee Tyson Airport, which moved from crowded Sutherland Avenue to Blount County in 1937. Author's Collection

At the end of World War II, a new era in medicine began. To explore the uses of radioactive isotopes in diagnosis and treatment, The University of Tennessee Memorial Research Center and Hospital was built on Alcoa Highway. Author's Collection

I. C. King Park was icy on February 16, 1966. Alcoa Highway overpasses the narrow boat channel linking this embayment to Fort Loudon Lake. Knoxville News-Sentinel

Solar energy was a burning question in 1975, when these experimental solar houses were built beside Alcoa Highway by The University of Tennessee. After the 1982 World's Fair closed, the largest windmill from the Australian Pavilion was relocated here to represent another kind of natural energy. Knoxville News-Sentinel

The Loudon Lake Dogwood Trail is famous for sheltered beauty spots that alternate with sweeping views. Dogwood Arts Festival

This home at 3512 Maloney Road, typifies Knox County's spacious and comfortable farmhouses of the 1870s. MPC Survey

First the Cherokees and then the gypsies built their campfires on the "river bluffs" overlooking downtown Knoxville. The tree-shaded vantage point was lowered and leveled for the construction of East Tennessee Baptist Hospital in 1948. Author's Collection

The Henley Bridge is featured on this 1937 souvenir plate that pictures the principal attractions in and around Knox County. Author's Collection

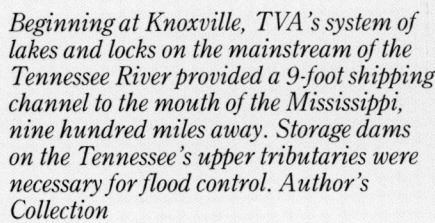

The width of the Tennessee River has not changed at all since the Henley Street Bridge was built in 1932; but the water level, controlled by downstream Fort Loudoun Dam, no longer rises after every rain or falls to this extent in periods of prolonged drought. Tennessee Valley Authority

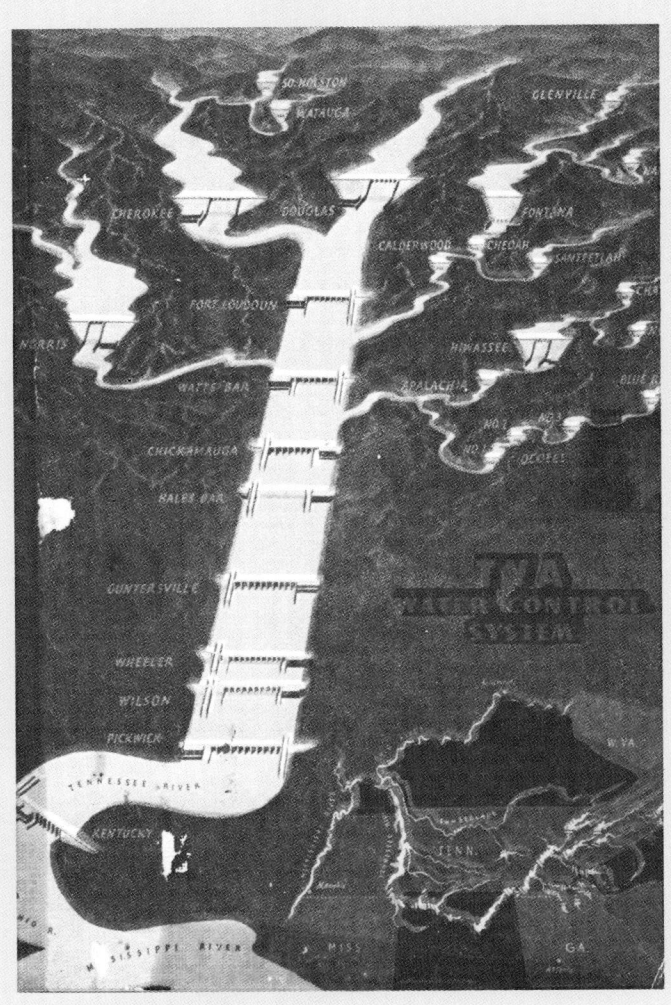

Beginning at Knoxville, TVA's system of lakes and locks on the mainstream of the Tennessee River provided a 9-foot shipping channel to the mouth of the Mississippi, nine hundred miles away. Storage dams on the Tennessee's upper tributaries were necessary for flood control. Author's Collection

Constant dredging is necessary to maintain TVA's 9-foot shipping channel that links Knox County with the Gulf of Mexico, now 450 miles away via the Tennessee-Tombigbee Waterway. Greater Knoxville Chamber of Commerce

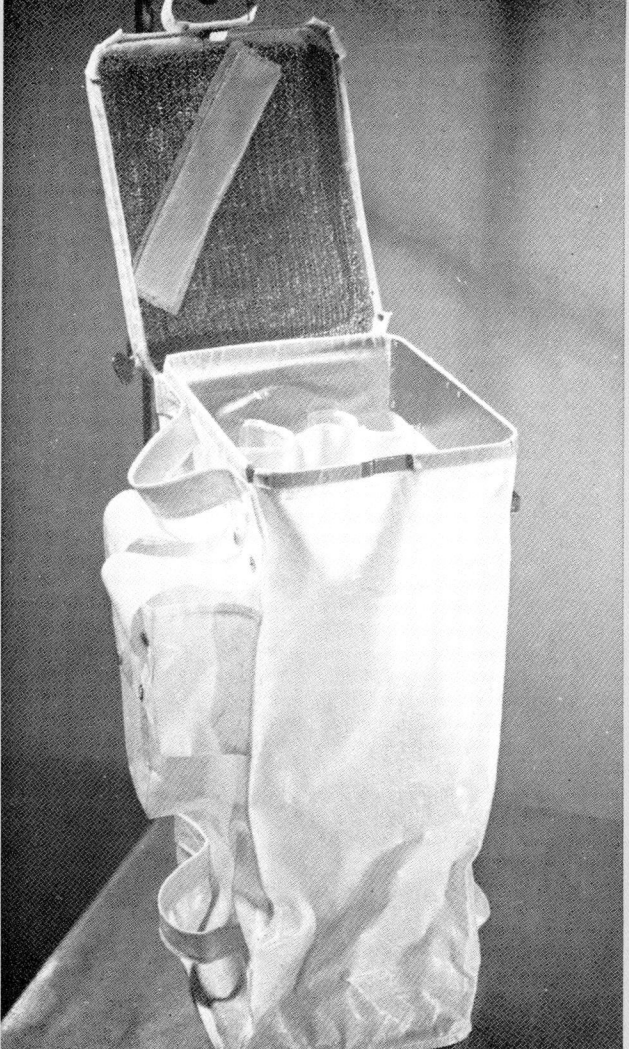

How far is it to the moon? This teflon bag began the five hundred thousand mile round trip from Blount Avenue in 1970, when the Knoxville Glove Company constructed improved carriers for the surface rocks and core samples collected by Apollo 13 astronauts. Courtesy of Rodman Townsend, Sr.

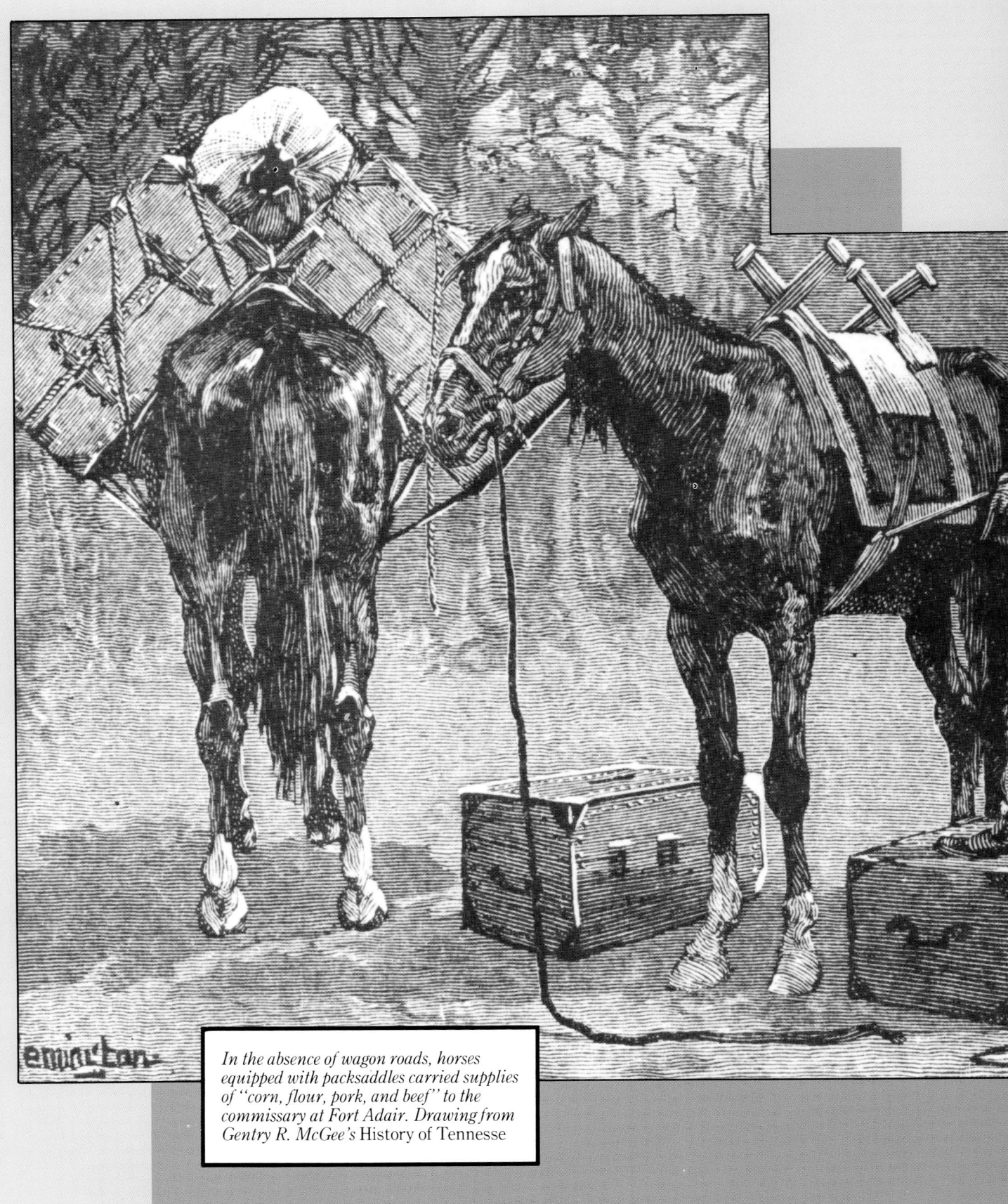

In the absence of wagon roads, horses equipped with packsaddles carried supplies of "corn, flour, pork, and beef" to the commissary at Fort Adair. Drawing from Gentry R. McGee's History of Tennesse

Chapter 3

North Knox County

In 1779, Col. Evan Shelby literally launched an expedition against a "scorpions' nest" of renegade Indians and white outlaws who had taken over five Cherokee towns near Mussel Shoals. His five hundred Virginia and North Carolina militiamen mustered at the edge of the forest near present-day Rogersville, where they felled great trees and made enough dugout canoes to transport themselves down the Holston and Tennessee rivers. After surprising and scattering the early-day terrorists, Shelby's men returned on foot, blazing a trail northeastward from the Emory River to the Holston. This wilderness trace became an important link in the first overland route to Nashville, and it still exists—as Emory Road.

Seven years later, John Adair built a two-story log house and a stockade on his 640-acre land grant that encompassed future Smithwood and Fountain City. In 1789, Fort Adair became the supply depot for the Cumberland Guards who accompanied groups of settlers on their dangerous journey down the Emory Road to Middle Tennessee. So well did John Adair fulfill his responsibilities as commissary that he was appointed one of the three town commissioners when Knoxville was laid out in 1791. He also served as a justice of the peace for Knox County, a trustee of Blount College, a member of Tennessee's constitutional convention, and a founding elder of both Lebanon-in-the-Fork and First Presbyterian churches.

Isolated cabins had appeared on two of North Knox County's ridges, Beaver and Bull Run, in 1785; and by 1792, enough settlers had moved into the nearby valleys to warrant the building of Bull Blockhouse for their protection.

The Powell area's first settler was John Manefee, who had already served as speaker of the house of representatives for the Lost State of Franklin and would later hold the same office under the state of Tennessee. Manefee's Station, built about 1787, was the largest fortified outpost in North Knox County, and when the Cherokee of the Lower Towns declared war on the United States in 1792, a captain of militia and fourteen men were assigned to protect the families "forting" there. The station's marked site is near Bell's Bridge, on the Old Clinton Highway.

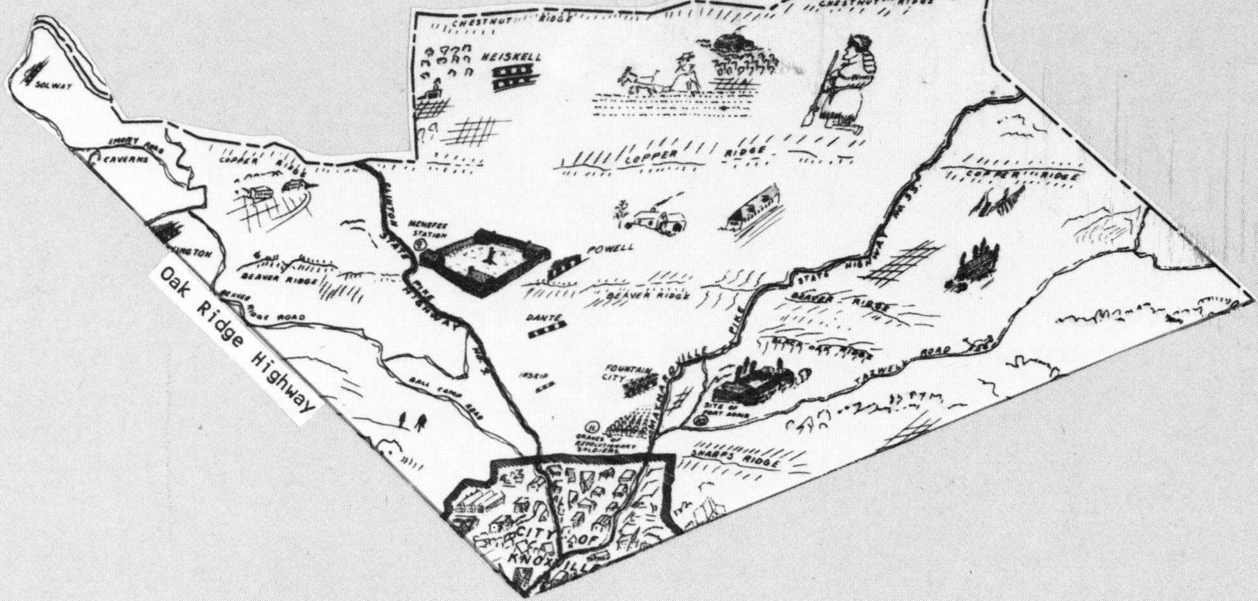

Nicholas Gibbs, who built this substantial house near Harbison's Crossroads in 1793, is the ancestor of many substantial citizens including William Gibbs McAdoo, President Woodrow Wilson's secretary of the treasury and son-in-law.

The house has been restored, and Gibbs descendants have organized a support group to ensure its preservation. "Historic Treasure Spots of Knox County"

The grave of George Mann (off Tazewell Pike, in the vicinity of Gibbs High School) as pictured in "Historic Treasure Spots of Knox County."

George Mann became Knox County's last victim of an Indian massacre on May 25, 1795, when he surprised a Creek raiding party at his barn. As the raiders then crept toward the nearby cabin, Indian file, Mrs. Mann saved her children's lives by wounding the first and second savages in line with a single rifle bullet, fired through a crack in the door.

The unique Cole-Harris house, built about 1800 on Washington Pike at Harris Road, has come down in the family of Simon Harris, a Revolutionary War veteran who owned large tracts of land in North Knox County, and lived to a vigorous old age.

In the 1950s, the Misses Delia, Bertie, and Mary Lou Harris appeared on national television, and confounded the panel on "I've Got a Secret" by announcing that their grandfather, at the age of twelve, served as a drummer boy in Gen. George Washington's army! Metropolitan Planning Commission's Historic Buildings Survey

Maryville College traces its origin to Murphy Road in North Knox County where, in 1802, the Reverend Isaac Anderson opened Union Academy. He moved his "log college" to Maryville in 1812, when he became pastor of New Providence Presbyterian Church.

Union Academy's most illustrious alumnus was Sam Houston, who lived with the Cherokee Indians for several years, taught school in Blount County, fought with Andrew Jackson in the Creek War, served in the U.S. Congress, and was governor of Tennessee—before he went to Texas. McClung Historical Collection

"Brickyard Farm," on Old Emory Road, was the home of Columbus Powell, for whom Powell's Station on a branch line of the East Tennessee, Virginia, and Georgia Railroad was named. It was for his daughter Lillie, Mrs. J. Allen Smith, that Knox County's all-time favorite White Lily Flour was named. MPC Survey

Frederick Steidinger Heiskell retired as publisher of the Knoxville Register *in 1837 to become a full-time farmer, and he was president of the Knox County Agricultural Society founded in 1850. As an early advocate of soil conservation, he insisted that Knox County's steep hillsides were ideally suited to fruit-farming; and by the 1870s, the flourishing orchards of the Heiskell Community had proved him right. McClung Historical Collection*

Beginning in the 1890s, dairying was a popular and profitable North Knox County enterprise. This neo-classic mansion, on the Sterchi Dairy Farm in Beaver Creek Valley, was built in 1912 by J.G. Sterchi who later headed the Sterchi chain of furniture stores. MPC Survey

Thomas Gray's "Elegy in a Country Churchyard" inspired the naming of a cemetery established in 1850 on North Broadway, outside the city limits.

Two United States senators, William G. Brownlow and Lawrence D. Tyson, are among the many notable Knox Countians buried at Old Gray. Photograph by Ron Childress for "Knoxville, Fifty Landmarks"

During the Civil War, a number of Union soldiers were buried in a special section of the Gray Cemetery. This area was afterward expanded into the National Cemetery, and given a separate entrance on Tyson Street. Author's Collection

Some years ago, Karns High School students researched the history of this house on Copper Ridge Road. They reported that it was built in 1834 by Reuben Fox, whose slaves found an ingenious way of making brick at a clay pit near the site. After a heavy rain, cattle were driven back and forth across the pit. Their hooves churned the clay to sticky mud, which was then pressed into wooden molds and placed in the sun to harden.

Professor Thomas Conner Karns, a native North Knox Countian for whom the High School is named, became the second superintendent of Knox County Schools in 1873. Within two years, he opened free public schools in every county district: one hundred for white and twenty-one for Negro pupils. *MPC Survey*

This house, to which Frances Hodgson moved from New Market with her widowed mother and sister, stood on what is now the Knoxville College campus. *Archives of Knoxville College*

English-born Frances Hodgson Burnett, the author of Little Lord Fauntleroy, lived in Knox County from 1869 to 1875, and during this time her short stories began to appear in print. She was married here in 1873 to Dr. Swan Burnett, whose appointment to the medical faculty of Georgetown University took them to Washington, D.C. *McClung Historical Collection*

When Knoxville College was established by the United Presbyterian Church in 1875, for the purpose of educating young black men and women for the ministerial and teaching professions, its grounds were scarred by Confederate siege-trenches dug in 1863. This plan of the campus, from a Travellers Protective Association publication of 1900, shows how the college had grown and prospered in its first twenty-five years.

In 1890, the U.S. Congress required all federal land-grant colleges to provide separate but equal facilities for white and negro students. From that time until 1909, when Tennessee A&I opened in Nashville, Knoxville College was a branch of the University of Tennessee, offering military training and courses in scientific agriculture.

In the late 1890s, KC cadets posed in front of the building erected to house the land-grant college program. Archives of Knoxville College

Curtis King, Harry Fields, Elijah Wells, and Edward Cothren are shown performing at the 1939 World's Fair in San Francisco, during their summer tour of thirty-six states and Mexico. The accompanist and director of the Senior Men's Quartet was Newell Coleridge Fitzpatrick, under whose leadership the music department of Knoxville College became one of the nation's finest. Knoxville College yearbook, The Knoxunior, *1940*

Mechanicsville was a bustling town, boasting several factories and a population of two thousand, when it was annexed to the city of Knoxville on its own petition in 1883. After a long period of decline, strenuous efforts have been made in recent years to rehabilitate its homes and rekindle community spirit. These silhouettes of typical structures illustrate the "Walking Tour of Mechanicsville" prepared by Knoxville Heritage, Inc.

About 1910, members of the National Federation of Negro Women's Clubs attended a tea at one of Mechanicsville's handsome homes. Beck Cultural Exchange Center

From 1840 until 1885, the area surrounding the Fountain Head Spring was used as a Methodist campground for "protracted meetings." Families came by wagon to the week-long revival services, bringing their own tents and food supplies. Author's Collection

From 1886 until it was destroyed by fire in 1920, the Fountain Head Hotel was the center of social life in the "summer resort" called Fountain City. During the off-season, it doubled as the Women's Residence Hall for Holbrook College. McClung Historical Collection

The Fountain Head Railway began operating on May 27, 1890. Its open-sided passenger cars were pulled by a "noiseless" dummy-engine. McClung Historical Collection

From its Knoxville terminal on Broadway opposite Emory Park, the Dummy Line's route followed Woodland Avenue past the present site of St. Mary's Hospital, continued through Lincoln Park and Arlington, and ended at this Fountain City station, on Broadway at Hotel Avenue. The round trip could be made in an hour. Author's Collection

Russell Briscoe's genre painting of Fountain City Park in its heyday. The Fountain Head Spring that gave the area its early name appears in the background, at right. Courtesy of the artist's daughter, Peggy Briscoe Rochelle. Photograph by Gary Heatherly

Then as now, heart-shaped Fountain City Lake was a pleasant place for an afternoon stroll.

The message on this 1907 postcard reads: "Dear Bess—we arrived all safe and sound, and having a delightful time. The location is ideal. Yours, Lillian." Author's Collection

Knox County's first courses in business management and secretarial skills were offered by Holbrook College, which opened in 1893, not far from the Fountain Head Hotel. Its orginal building burned in 1900, but was rebuilt. In 1906, the college property was purchased by Knox County and became Central High School. This photograph, from the 1897-98 college catalogue, was provided by the McClung Historical Collection

Central High School's outmoded structure was replaced by this "modern" building in 1931. It is now Gresham Middle School, named in honor of Central High's outstanding longtime principal, Miss Hassie K. Gresham. Author's Collection

Early night lighting on the Fountain City Dogwood Trail's beautiful Garden Side. In 1985, the Dogwood Arts Festival celebrated twenty-five blooming years by extending this trail across North Broadway, where the route on Black Oak Ridge is called the Panorama Side. Knoxville News-Sentinel

Magnificent "Belcaro" was built on the crest of Black Oak Ridge in 1912 by Judge Hugh L. McClung, in whose memory the McClung Plaza and Tower on the UT campus are named. MPC Survey

This Knoxville Journal *photograph shows guests enjoying a Ballet Benefit in Belcaro's garden, given in support of the Fountain City Library. UTK Special Collections Library*

Ellen McClung Berry's sponsorship of the arts and personal involvement in historic preservation have changed Knox County for the better. She is pictured beside Belcaro's colonnade. UTK Special Collections Library

In 1833, Col. Joseph Scott ordered hand-painted scenic wallpaper from Paris for the parlor of his new "country" home that stands near Broadway on Oglewood Avenue (Stevens Mortuary). When Colonel Scott's house became a church in 1946, Mrs. Thomas Berry (Ellen McClung) saw to it that the colorful paper was removed and carefully preserved. It now ornaments the dining room walls at "Crescent Bend" on Kingston Pike. "Historic Treasure Spots of Knox County"

This first house on Scott Street, and the nucleus of the neighborhood known as Old North Knoxville, was the residence of Francis A. R. Scott.

On a sunny day in 1888, the calash-hood of the family carriage was folded back; a top hat was proper attire for the coachman of so elegant an equipage. The Story of Two Chairs

Like a public building at the end of a mall, the turn-of-the-century residence of J. M. Dunn still faces Armstrong Avenue, in Old North Knoxville. Commercial History of Tennessee

"Greystone," now the headquarters of WATE-TV, was built on North Broadway by Maj. Eldod Cicero Camp in 1890, for the then astronomical sum of $125,000. UTK Special Collections Library

In the 1890s, "rapid transit" meant a horse-drawn streetcar, like the one that halted long enough in front of the stylish Albert Greenwood residence on Washington Avenue for Drury E. Webb to take this photograph. Courtesy of the Greenwoods' granddaughter, Juliana Nickerson

Victor Ashe opened his successful 1987 campaign for mayor of Knoxville with a rally on Luttrell Street, in the turn-of-the-century Fourth and Gill Neighborhood. Knoxville News-Sentinel photograph by Michael Patrick

Beginning in 1910, students from all parts of the city converged on Knoxville High School, which graduated its last class in 1951. Before Knoxville schools were turned over to Knox County in 1987, city schools administration occupied the block-square brick building on Fifth Avenue.

This postcard-drawing, which went on sale before the high school opened, is signed "Baumann Bros. Architects." Author's Collection

In the early twentieth century, two large hospitals faced each other across narrow Cleveland Place. On the west side was the publicly-owned Knoxville General Hospital. The Knox County Health Department Center occupies this site, and a former hospital annex on Wray Street is now Serene Manor Medical Center. Commercial History of Tennessee

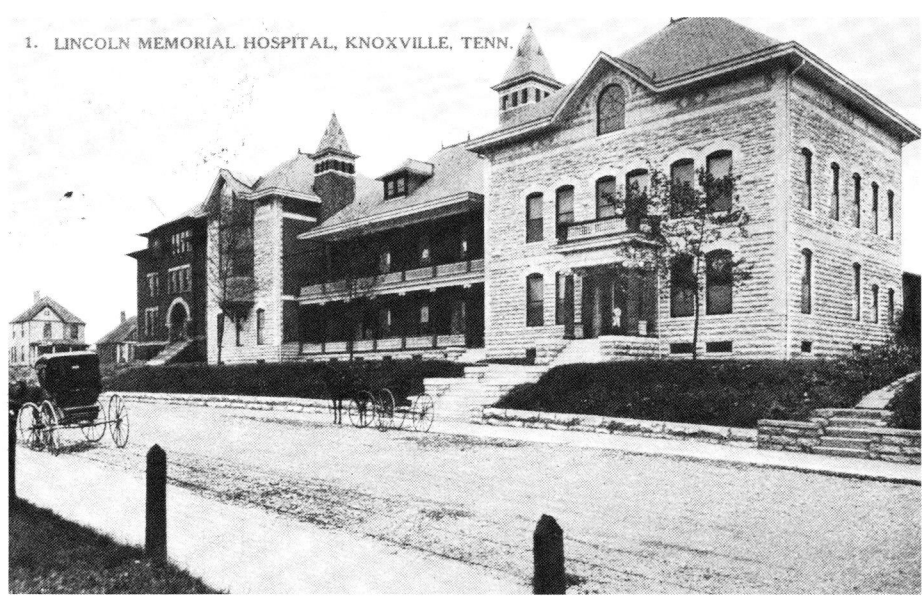

On the east side of Cleveland Place stood Lincoln Memorial Hospital for private patients. Author's Collection

North Knoxville, separated from downtown by a railroad-filled ravine, was made easier to reach in 1919 when a previous narrow bridge was supplanted by the present Gay Street Viaduct. While the viaduct was under construction, trestles supported the one-way temporary road and two-way streetcar tracks. McClung Historical Collection

In the 1920s, Whittle Springs Hotel was Knox County's most prestigious year-round "resort," complete with a large spring-fed swimming pool and an eighteen hole golf course that is now city-owned. Mineral water from its natural springs was sold in huge five-gallon bottles, throughout the Knoxville area. Knoxville News-Sentinel

Because its original wooden structure had been destroyed by fire, the new stuccoed-brick hotel was the first in this area to be protected by a sprinkler system. During a memorable Fourth of July banquet, diners were drenched when a tossed firecracker set off the dining room's overhead sprinklers. Author's collection

After Whittle Springs Hotel was purchased by Radio Station WNOX, and replaced by a new broadcasting studio, a station-sponsored Easter egg hunt drew crowds of children and parents to the hotel's former front lawn in 1956. The pavilion at left in this Knoxville News-Sentinel *photograph covered the five wells that tapped the underground mineral springs, and the small nearby building was the bottling plant for "Whittle Water."*

Tuberculosis was a major cause of death in Knox County until the 1920s when Beverly Hills Sanitarium was established by Dr. Herbert Acuff with the aid of the Civitan Club. Fresh air and bed rest over a period of months saved many lives there, but now that "miracle drugs" provide a speedy cure for TB, the sanitarium has become the county's Hillcrest Beverly Nursing Home. UTK Special Collections Library

Since it was established by the Sisters of Mercy in 1930, St. Mary's Hospital on Oakwood Avenue has grown from a single structure to a building complex covering several blocks. Greater Knoxville Chamber of Commerce

"COMMUNITY NITE" LONSDALE

Lonsdale, the close-knit community that grew up around the Patent Button Company and the Knoxville Iron Works, became a part of Knoxville in 1917. A local jazz band provided entertainment for "Community Nite" in the 1920s. McClung Historical Collection

Ivan Racheff, a noted metallurgist who headed the Knoxville Iron Company for many years, turned a slag heap into a showplace garden on the company's grounds. The Knox County Council of Garden Clubs now owns and maintains the lovely Racheff Gardens on Tennessee Avenue in Lonsdale. Knoxville News-Sentinel

Callahan Road takes its name from this North Knox County showplace of the early 1900s, the home of George W. Callahan. Cardinal Gibbons was the Callahans' houseguest in 1913, when he delivered the Columbus Day address at the National Conservation Exposition. First Exposition of Conservation and Its Builders

In the days when roads were few and far between, crossroads were ideal locations for country stores like the one owned by the Hall family on Emory Road at Maynardville Pike.

The transformation of sleepy Halls Crossroads into the wide-awake Halls Community began in the 1930s, when the Norris Freeway was built for access to the construction site of Norris Dam. Author's Collection

President and Mrs. Franklin D. Roosevelt arrived for an official visit of inspection to Norris Dam in 1934. Escorted by TVA Board Chairman Arthur E. Morgan, they made the round trip from Knoxville in this open touring car. Tennessee Valley Authority

They saw the Clinch River, struggling through the gaps in partially completed Norris Dam. Tennessee Valley Authority

Sharp's Ridge Park, which opened in 1953, was paid for by public subscription as a memorial to veterans of all wars. Area garden clubs were not slow to accept the challenge of beautifying its many acres, and this 1963 photograph from the Knoxville News-Sentinel *shows a determined crew at work on roadside planting.*

Seen from Sharp's Ridge, North Knoxville looked like this before the coming of the interstates. The Southern Railway's Coster Shops are on the right in this photograph by Bill Tracey.

Knox County's most famous Indian massacre occurred on September 25, 1793, in the Walker Springs area. Several hundred Cherokee and Creek warriors, led by John Watts and Doublehead, were on their way to attack Knoxville when they heard the distant boom of the sunrise cannon at the U.S. Army's Blockhouse Fort. Unwilling to face the Fort's artillery fire, the war party turned aside to tiny, isolated Cavett's Station where they killed and mutilated the thirteen members of Alexander Cavett's family and burned the fortified log cabin to the ground. Drawing from McGee's History of Tennessee

Chapter 4

WEST KNOX COUNTY

Ever since 1783, West Knox County's waterfront has attracted homeowners and developers. In that year, James White and Francis Alexander Ramsey were among the prospective investors who explored the north shore of the Tennessee River as far as an area they christened "Grassy Valley," which extended westward from Ten Mile Creek past the present county line. James White's son-in-law, Charles McClung, and Francis Ramsey's brother, the Reverend S. G. Ramsey, would one day be prominent Grassy Valley residents, but they were not the first. The name "Ebenezer" commemorates the vicinity's original settler, Ebenezer Byram, who built a cabin there in 1785.

The settlement of two nearby valleys also began in 1785. One was Hardin Valley, where Col. Joseph Hardin of Virginia owned two thousand acres on Silver Creek. The other was lower Hind's Valley, where Wells' Station was West Knox County's best fortified outpost.

A Grassy Valley trading post started in 1787 by Robertus Love became a thriving hamlet with a tannery, a rope-walk, a smithy, and a cobbler's shop. Loveville declined and disappeared but its location is still pinpointed on the map—where its namesake "Lovell Road" ends at Kingston Pike.

Far more important and enduring was the settlement that grew up on Turkey Creek where, in 1787, Col. David Campbell of Virginia built a blockhouse fort. Colonel Campbell's "station" was a welcome stopping place on the perilous route to Middle Tennessee, and its attractions soon included two taverns, a tannery, a wagon factory, and a cabinet-maker's shop, as well as a general store. In 1792, the first Knox County Court employed Charles McClung to survey and build a good road westward from the county seat at Knoxville to the county line at Kingston, and Campbell's Station was the halfway point on the new Kingston Pike.

In September of 1792, the Cherokee of the Lower Towns formally declared war on the United States, and the territorial militia was called out: a corporal and six men were posted at Wells' Station to protect the families taking shelter there. In the months that followed, Indians often lay in wait outside the fort, for solitary settlers.

Nicholas Ball, a hunter and trapper living at the end of the road that is still called Ball Camp Pike, was ambushed three times and twice escaped uninjured but with bullet holes in his hat. He was then waylaid and killed while bringing a load of corn to the hungry refugees at Wells' Station.

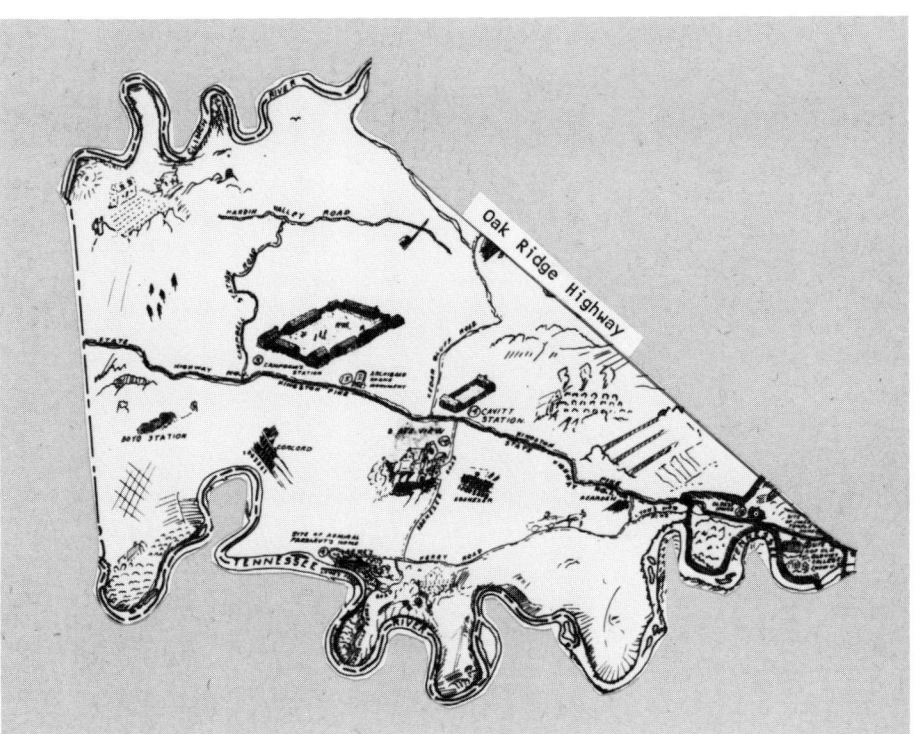

In 1792, the first Knox County Court employed Charles McClung to build the Kingston Pike. He, in turn, hired Thomas Hope to design and build a fine house overlooking the new road. "Statesview," begun in 1804, was so named because it commanded a double panorama of the Smokies beyond whose crest lay North Carolina, and the Cumberlands, where settlement then ended on the Middle Tennessee plateau.

After the death of Charles McClung in 1835, the property was purchased by Frederick S. Heiskell who planted orchards on the hillsides, and re-named the house "Fruit Hill." "Historic Treasure Spots of Knox County"

Charles McClung and his wife Margaret (the eldest daughter of James White, Knoxville's founder) were the parents of nine children and the progenitors of many prominent Knox countians. Their daughter Polly was one of the first five coeds at Blount College in 1804.

This delightful silhouette is from the Ellen McClung Berry Collection, a part of the McClung Historical Collection

"Glenmary," on Ebenezer Road, was built about 1830 by Dennis McCoughan on property settled in 1797 by Rev. Samuel G. Ramsey. The Reverend Ramsey, who was the organizer and pastor of two nearby Presbyterian churches, also found time to conduct Ebenezer Academy, a "classical school for young gentlemen." His wife presided over a similar school for girls, known as "The Parsonage." Photograph by Ron Childress

Scholarly Judge Archibald Roane, who lived in Grassy Valley, was elected governor of Tennessee in 1801, when the state constitution required John Sevier to step down after three consecutive terms in office. He served until 1803, when Sevier defeated him for reelection.

Tennessee's second governor is buried in Pleasant Forest Cemetery on Concord Road. His grave remained unmarked until 1919, when the state belatedly erected this monument on the one hundredth anniversary of his death. McClung Historical Collection

Adm. George Dewey visited Knoxville in 1900 to dedicate this marker erected by Bonny Kate Chapter of the Daughters of the American Revolution at the site of Adm. David Farragut's birthplace. The spot is now a peninsula jutting into Fort Loudoun Lake. Photograph by James C. Thompson

Adm. David Glasgow Farragut was born on July 5, 1801, at Stoney Point, later called Lowe's Ferry, where his father, George Farragut, owned a large farm and operated a ferry on the Tennessee River.

David Farragut became the first admiral in the United States Navy. That rank was especially created for him after the Civil War battle of Mobile Bay, at which his rallying cry was "Damn the torpedoes—Full speed ahead!" UTK Special Collections Library

What's in a name?

Middlebrook Pike originally led to "Middlebrook," which increases in beauty with the passing years. The house was designed and built (circa 1845) by Gideon Morgan Hazen, whose business partner and cousin was Marcus DeLafayette Bearden, for whom the Bearden Community was named. Until 1886, the partners owned and operated the nearby steam-assisted, water-powered paper factory at the end of Papermill Road. Photograph by Bruce Gibbins, 1935

In 1824, Col. David Campbell sold his station to Samuel Martin, who opened Knox County's first race track there within a year. By 1835, trade was so brisk that Martin added this brick annex onto the original log inn that had been patronized by such notable guests as John Sevier and Andrew Jackson. After Campbell's Station was by-passed by the railroad in the 1850s, and passenger trains made stagecoaches obsolete, the inn at the corner of Kingston Pike and Campbell's Station Road became the residence of Avery Russell. *"Historic Treasure Spots of Knox County"*

Farragut, Knox County's newest municipality, celebrated Tennessee Homecoming '86 with a reenactment of the Civil War Battle of Campbell's Station alongside Turkey Creek. The combat was photographed by Dave Carter, for the Knoxville News-Sentinel.

On the morning of the actual battle in 1863, Union General Hartranft had breakfast at the nearby Avery Russell house; Confederate General McLaws arrived in time for supper. Between meals, the Russell family retired to the basement, taking with them a valuable white horse that they managed to hide from both armies!

Nationally acclaimed architect John Russell Pope designed this elegant neo-classical residence in 1915 for the H.L. Dulin family. Before the Knoxville Art Museum was relocated on the Fair Site, the house served for twenty years as the Dulin Gallery of Art. Its permanent collection included nine of the famous miniature rooms created by Mrs. James Ward Thorne. Knoxville Convention and Visitors Bureau

Next door, the residence and grounds once owned by federal judge George C. Taylor provided space for the Dulin Gallery's extra-curricular activities. In 1988, both houses became outposts of nearby Calvary Baptist Church. Courtesy of Mitchell Taylor

123

The tea-house in the water-garden was a special feature of the Sanford Arboretum, landscaped early in this century by the Olmstead Brothers of Brookline, Massachusetts. The Arboretum, which contained hundreds of native and exotic trees and shrubs, was the hobby of Alfred Sanford, Sr., whose Kingston Pike residence now provides additional space for the First United Methodist Church. Photograph by James Thompson, 1935

Knoxville's first planned subdivision, Sequoyah Hills, is named for a Native American born a few miles away in a Cherokee town on the Little Tennessee River. This portrait of Sequoyah shows him with the great invention that made him famous: a phonetic alphabet that enabled all Indian tongues to become written languages. Reproduced from This Is Tennessee, *by Mary U. Rothrock*

Because America's tallest native trees bear the name of the alphabet's inventor, a Sequoia gigantea *was planted on the Indian Mound in the centerstrip of Cherokee Boulevard in 1976 to commemorate the nation's Bicentennial. Photograph by Charles Tichy for Knoxville Heritage*

This English manor house, built of native limestone for Mr. and Mrs. Charles Moore, was one of the earliest homes on Cherokee Boulevard. It was purchased in 1987 by the Pulitzer prize-winning author, Alex Haley. Photograph by Bruce Gibbins, 1935

TVA's flowage easement along Cherokee Boulevard is leased by the city of Knoxville for lakeside Sequoyah Park. Greater Knoxville Chamber of Commerce

No houses overlooked Talahi's Mountain Lion Fountain when this photograph was taken by James Thompson, and a treeless Papoose Park appears at right. Talahi Mall's architectural use of Cherokee symbols earned it a listing on the National Register.

Papoose Park, designed as an enclosed children's playground, has unique wrought-iron gates bearing the Cherokee symbol for protection, the thunderbird.

Several years ago, to the distress of Talahi residents, the gates mysteriously disappeared. A determined search discovered them at a city-owned swimming pool, hanging upside down! Photograph by Charles Tichy, for Knoxville Heritage, Inc.

The very first Dogwood Trail, which opened here in 1955, proved John Gunther was wrong when he called Knoxville "America's ugliest city" in his Inside USA.

Night-lighted Dogwood Trails began on Towanda Trail in 1957, when six members of the Knoxville Garden Club experimented with bare bulbs, indoor extension cords, and aluminum pie-plate reflectors. A sudden shower shorted out electricity in all of Sequoyah Hills! Knoxville News-Sentinel

About 1809, Capt. William Lyon purchased a large tract of land overlooking a horseshoe bend of the Tennessee River with four tiers of smoke-blue mountains in the distance; and ever since, the area has been known as Lyons View. Author's Collection

The official title of this mental hospital established in 1883 was the East Tennessee Insane Asylum, but its euphemistic local name was "Lyons View." It is now called Lakeshore Mental Health Center. Author's Collection

Cherokee Country Club was built at the midpoint of the river's horseshoe bend in 1907, across Lyons View Pike from its eighteen hole golf course—Knox County's first. In the 1909 photograph, stylish "autos" fill the parking area, and a lady member practices on the putting green. Courtesy of Cherokee Country Club

Cherokee was called "the South's finest Country Club" in the 1920s when this elegant facility replaced the original wooden clubhouse. Author's Collection

Hilltop condominiums echo the Moorish architecture of this castle built in 1928 by Weston M. Fulton. Before achieving fame and fortune as an inventor, he had headed Knoxville's Weather Bureau. UTK Special Collections Library

The invitation to Westmoreland Dogwood Trail's 1988 opening pictured the waterwheel built on Fourth Creek by Judge Clary Webb to provide power for the area's first homes. Drawing by Doug Griffith

Not all of West Knox County's lakes were created by TVA. Dead Horse Lake was formed by accident in 1910, when a horse strayed into a marshy area and drowned. Its carcass had blocked the natural outlet of a little stream, but the lake did not disappear after the obstruction was removed. To be sure of preserving this natural phenomenon, the property's owner sealed the drain hole in the cave cap with cement.
Scenic Resources of the Tennessee Valley

A bit of Merrie Olde England? No, this Tudor structure on Gray-Hendrix Road in Byington was built in 1927—of railroad ties! MPC Survey

W-121—A View of one of the Process Buildings and Cooling Towers in the Foreground, Clinton Engineer Works, Oak Ridge, Tenn., "City of the Atomic Bomb"

Suddenly, in 1942, the Solway Bridge ended at a high fence on the Anderson County side of the Clinch River, and armed guards turned away all but "authorized personnel." Behind the fence, in deepest secrecy, the first atomic chain-reactor was placed in operation on November 4, 1943. Author's Collection

Hundreds of "flat-tops" provided housing for the town that mushroomed out of raw red clay just across the Clinch River from West Knox County. For a brief time, Oak Ridge, with seventy-five thousand inhabitants, was Tennessee's fifth largest city. Author's Collection

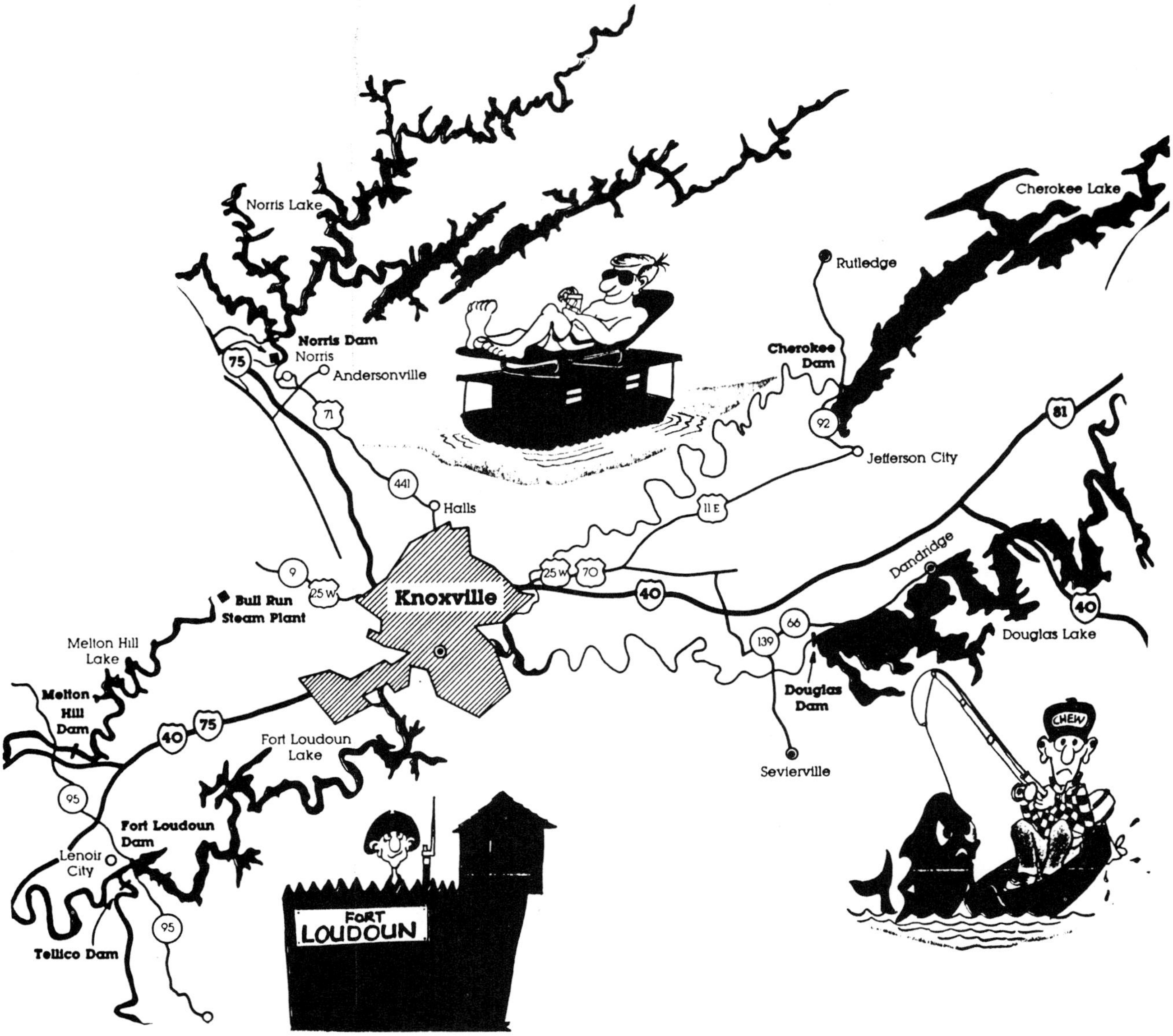

Six of TVA's "Great lakes of the South" are within thirty-five miles of the Authority's downtown Knoxville headquarters, and two of these—Fort Loudoun and Melton Hill—enclose West Knox County like parentheses. Tennessee Valley Authority

Riverside roads and farms of West Knox County were inundated in 1943 by Fort Loudoun Dam, which rose 130 feet above the riverbed and contained the highest single-lift lock in the world. Author's Collection

In 1854, a brand new town called "Concord" sprang up beside the tracks of the East Tennessee & Georgia Railroad. As the shipping point for fine marble from nearby quarries, it became the most populous community in West Knox County.

When the waters of Fort Loudoun Lake inundated the Tennessee River's shoreline, the Concord area lost all its quarries and half a town, but gained Knox County's largest park. TVA furnished this aerial overview of Concord Park on its opening day, May 15, 1959 to the Knoxville News-Sentinel.

Carl Cowan Park, which also offers swimming, tennis, and watersports, is named for a prominent black attorney. Its use was originally limited to members of his race. Photograph by Michael Patrick for the Knoxville News-Sentinel

Fort Loudoun Lake brought the wonders of watersports to Knox County. Greater Knoxville Chamber of Commerce

West Knox County is bordered on the north by TVA's Melton Hill Lake. College crews come from all parts of the country to practice rowing on its smooth surface, unruffled by strong winds. Knoxville Convention and Visitors Bureau

Farragut, Knox County's newest incorporated township, is a recent outgrowth of historic Campbell's Station. There, modern day residents will preserve the pioneer heritage of Grassy Valley with a Folklife Museum in the clapboarded-log Neuhauser home, moved from the Pellissippi Parkway area. Photograph by Jack Kirkland for the Knoxville News-Sentinel

For exactly two hundred years after its first settlement, Hardin Valley was a peaceful farming community. Resettlement of a different kind began in 1985, with the building of a new campus for State Technical Institute of Knoxville, which became Pellissippi State Technical Community College in 1988. Knoxville News-Sentinel

Until the 1920s, The Hill was the entire campus of The University of Tennessee. Then the College of Home Economics was built on the site of "Sunnyside," the longtime home of the Hugh A. M. White and Thomas Rodgers families. The white frame house was built about 1810 by Pleasant M. Miller, who had married Governor Blount's daughter, Mary Louisa.

All of what is now the Fort Sanders Neighborhood was owned by Hugh Andrew May White. The property, which included the Civil War fort, was subdivided by his heirs in the 1870s, and was known as "White's Addition." McClung Historical Collection

Once upon a time, there were fairy tale castles....

Deep trenches dug by Union soldiers in 1863 fill the foreground of this rare photograph taken from Fort Sanders, which offers a rear view of the first residence in White's Addition. When James D. Cowan built his house in 1880, he included a water tower for indoor plumbing and added a double "glass conservatory."

At left beyond it are the W. P. Chamberlain home on Cumberland Avenue and Tyson House, which was then a white frame "country place." "Melrose" appears in the distance, on the right. UTK Special Collections Library

In 1900, the Cowan residence was purchased by Daniel Briscoe, Sr., whose family enjoyed its "vestibule" front door, and the full-length bowling alley in the basement, until 1920 when it was sold to the university. Sophronia Strong and Clement Halls now occupy the "Briscoe block," but the carriage house and the servants' quarters are still standing. Courtesy of Nancy McMillan Rodgers

Brig. Gen. Lawrence D. Tyson, a graduate of West Point, came to Knoxville as the university's commandant of cadets and stayed on to become an illustrious citizen. As a colonel in the Spanish-American War, he commanded the Sixth U.S. Volunteers and served as military governor of Puerto Rico; as a general in World War I, he commanded the Thirtieth Division, which broke Germany's Hindenburg Line to enter Belgium. He was elected to the U.S. Senate in 1925. UT Magazine, Historical Edition

The parlor of the Tysons' large frame residence on Temple Avenue was the "acme of elegance and the height of fashion" in 1902. Some Representative Women of Tennessee

In 1907, the Tysons' home was faced with brick, and embellished with two classical porticoes and a porte-cochere. Tyson House, the only castle still surviving, is the headquarters of the Knoxville campus Alumni Association and houses the UTK Development Office. Author's Collection

Tyson Park, located where Cumberland Avenue becomes Kingston Pike at Third Creek, was given to the city of Knoxville in 1929 by Mrs. Lawrence D. Tyson on condition that the municipal airport forever bear the name of her son, Naval Lt. McGhee Tyson, the first flying officer killed in World War I. The first night lighting on the tennis courts was installed in 1960. Greater Knoxville Chamber of Commerce

"Melrose," built by John J. Craig in the 1850s, was subsequently owned by Judge Oliver P. Temple (for whom Temple Avenue was named) and by Thomas O'Conner. In this century, it housed the Melrose Art Center, and the Melrose residential district was developed on its once-extensive grounds. Hess Hall stands on its hilltop site.

In 1976, friends of Mr. and Mrs. Russell Briscoe received this Christmas card, a line-reproduction of his "Melrose" painting. Courtesy of Nancy McMillan Rodgers

"Melrose" was the childhood home of Miss Mary Boyce Temple, who chose this picture of herself in 1902 for inclusion in Some Representative Women of Tennessee, by Annie S. Gilchrist.

Mary Boyce Temple was the first president of Ossoli Circle, the South's oldest women's club, founded in 1885 and named for an early-day feminist, Margaret Fuller Ossoli. In 1893, Miss Mary established Knox County's first DAR Chapter, named "Bonny Kate" for Tennessee's first "first lady," the wife of Gov. John Sevier. Gov. Benton McMillin appointed Miss Mary to represent the state of Tennessee at the Paris Exposition of 1900, and in 1921, Lincoln Memorial University awarded her an honorary LL.D. degree. In 1925, she gave her personal check for an option on endangered Blount Mansion, and led the fight to purchase and restore what has been called "the most historic site in Tennessee."

For half a century, the wrought-iron balconies and gabled turrets of the W. W. Woodruff mansion overlooked the entrance to The University of Tennessee campus.

When the property was purchased and cleared by the University in 1930, the carriage house was allowed to remain. Tucked away behind Hoskins Library, it is now an experimental textiles laboratory for the College of Human Ecology, where plastic containers are re-cycled into cloth by "melt-blowing." UT Center for Educational Video and Photography

The trees chopped down before the Battle of Fort Sanders never grew back, and the hillside was still perfectly bare in the early 1920s, when Fort Sanders Hospital opened in its original building on the Civil War fortification's site. Empty Cumberland Avenue is in the foreground. McClung Historical Collection

When Fort Sanders Neighborhood Association celebrated the nation's Bicentennial with a street fair on Laurel Avenue, local history was represented by the dignified M.L. Ross house in the background. East Tennessee Community Design Center

The spacious Clinch Street residence of Professor W. W. Carson, taking on a new look in 1984 for its new identity as Ronald MacDonald House, a home away from home for the families of small patients at East Tennessee Children's Hospital. Knoxville News-Sentinel

Missing from Highland Avenue is this house immortalized by James Agee in A Death in the Family. *UT Center for Educational Video and Photography*

Geographically, the Eleventh Street Artists' Colony adjoins the World's Fair Site. Architecturally, the areas are a century apart. East Tennessee Community Design Center

America's first non-sectarian college was chartered by America's first territorial legislature, which met in Knoxville in 1794, and named for the territory's governor, William Blount. In 1797, Blount College moved into this handsome new building at the corner of Gay and Clinch streets that was paid for by public subscription. The drawing, signed M. Nesseter, hangs in the Chancellor's suite at Blount College's lineal descendant, The University of Tennessee, Knoxville

Chapter 5

A City Within The City— The University Of Tennessee

History was made here in 1804, when America's first coeds were enrolled at Blount College. Portraits of the five pioneers were photographed by Miles Wright at the Frank H. McClung Museum on the campus of The University of Tennessee.

Barbara Blount was born in Knoxville in 1792, and Blount Mansion was her childhood home. She was orphaned at the age of ten by the death of Gov. William Blount in 1800, and Mary Grainger Blount in 1802. She lived in the home of her sister Mary Louisa (Mrs. Pleasant M. Miller) while attending the college named for her father. She moved with the Millers to "Sunnyside" on Cumberland Avenue, where she was married in 1815 to Gen. Edmund Pendleton Gaines, a hero of the War of 1812.

This twentieth-century portrait was painted by Mary E. Grainger, a well-known Knox County artist.

Jane Crozier (Jenny) Armstrong was the daughter of (Trooper) James Armstrong, the master of ceremonies at the Holston Treaty Meeting, and his wife, Susan Wells; the family home was near Brice's Bridge in East Knox County. After her marriage in 1809 to William Park, a prosperous Knoxville merchant, she lived in a Palladian brick house that stood on downtown Cumberland Avenue until the 1920s.

This original portrait of Jenny Armstrong, by an unknown artist, was presented to The University of Tennessee by her descendants.

Polly McClung's parents were Charles McClung, who surveyed and planned the city of Knoxville in 1791, and his wife Margaret, the eldest daughter of James White, the city's founder. After attending Blount College, she completed her education at Salem Academy in Winston-Salem, North Carolina. In 1811, she was married at "Statesview" to Thomas Lanier Williams, who became the first chancery judge for eighteen East Tennessee counties.

This portrait is by Edward Hurst, a Knoxville native who became a "court painter" in London after World War II.

Mattie and Kittie Kain were the daughters of John and Mary McMullen Kain whose home, "Trafalgar," was designed and built by Thomas Hope. Its site at Kain's Bend on the Holston River is now part of the Southern Railway's John Sevier Yards.

The elder sister, Mattie, was married in 1808. Her husband, Robert King, began the family tradition of steamboat ownership, and was the treasurer of Knoxville's first subscription library in 1817.

She is represented in the university's collection by this copy of a mid-nineteenth century portrait.

Kittie Kain was married in 1813 to Enoch Parsons (a library subscriber) who was elected city alderman in 1818.

Mary E. Grainger, herself a descendant of Jenny Armstrong, was well versed in history. She painted this idealized childish portrait of Kittie Kain as a reminder that Blount College followed the custom of American colleges in the early nineteenth century by admitting students at the age of twelve.

In 1806, Blount College changed its name to East Tennessee College. In 1826 the college purchased "The Hill," and moved to this steepled structure which, after 1842, centered the handsome brick quadrangle of East Tennessee University. Old College survived the Union occupation and Confederate bombardment of the university during the Civil War. UTK Special Collections Library

Dr. Thomas W. Humes organized St. John's Episcopal Church in 1844, resigning as rector in 1867 to accept the presidency of East Tennessee University. He accomplished the restoration of the war-torn campus and the change from a classical college to a military school, and was still president of the institution when it became The University of Tennessee in 1879. He came out of retirement in 1886 to become the first head of Lawson McGhee Library. McClung Historical Collection

During the Siege of Knoxville in 1863, a photographer standing within the breastworks of Fort Sanders recorded this view of East Tennessee University for posterity. The college buildings were then occupied by Union troops and were frequently shelled by Confederate artillery from the heights across the river. UT Magazine, Historical Edition

After Tennessee was readmitted to the Federal Union in 1866, East Tennessee University was designated the state's land-grant college. In order to receive funds from the sale of public lands, the Land Grant Act required the university to become a military school. All students wore uniforms, and were called cadets. Rigid military discipline prevailed, and daily drills were held on the parade ground atop The Hill.

In 1917, compulsory military training was replaced by an ROTC program. *UTK Special Collections Library*

To satisfy the second requirement of the Land Grant Act, a large riverside farm was purchased in 1869 and courses in agriculture were included in the curriculum. A group of trees at right center marks the large Indian mound that is now surrounded by buildings of the College of Agriculture. *UT Magazine, Historical Edition*

By 1875, two new buildings had been added to the three that had survived the war. South College, the fourth building on the hilltop, and Estabrook Hall, at left, are still standing and in use. UTK Special Collections Library

These cadets lived in Old South College in 1890. Third from the left in the second row is James D. Hoskins, who was dean of the university for two decades before becoming its president in 1934. UT Center for Educational Video and Photography

America's first coeds were enrolled at Blount College in 1804, but the school changed its policy as well as its name when it moved from Gay Street to The Hill. Women were not readmitted to The University of Tennessee until 1893. UTK Special Collections Library

This tabletop model of the university campus, as seen from the river, was displayed in Nashville at the Tennessee Centennial in 1897.

Tennessee's hundredth birthday actually occurred in 1896, but the celebration had to be delayed a year because the centennial grounds in Nashville were not ready on time. UTK Special Collections Library

In 1902, Dr. Philander P. Claxton founded the Summer School of the South, for the expressed purpose of teaching teachers how to teach. He hoped to attract three hundred participants, but by the end of registration day, twelve hundred students had lined up to enroll. Open-sided temporary buildings were hastily constructed on the hilltop drill field, but students from flat country were so discouraged by the steep climb that Dr. Claxton provided "jitney-service" from Cumberland Avenue, with hired hacks. UT Magazine, Historical Edition

The "Dining Hall" could not accommodate all the students at one time, so meals were served in "sittings."

After the Summer School was discontinued in 1917. the university established a pioneering College of Education and extended the school year to include a full-curriculum summer term. UT Magazine, Historical Edition

High jinks at Halloween included hoisting a horse's skeleton and a wagon to the roof of Jefferson Hall. UT Magazine, Historical Edition

In 1918, Pres. Brown Ayres spent several weeks in Nashville, lobbying for the university's first major appropriation from the state of Tennessee. When the legislature approved his request for a $1,000,000 building fund, Dr. Ayres sent a telegram to Mrs. Ayres in Knoxville. It read "BILL PASSED. HALLELUJAH," and Western Union delivered it as a black-bordered death message!

One third of the appropriation was used to build Ayres Hall; the rest established the medical school in Memphis. UT Magazine, Historical Edition

Early in the 1920s, imposing Ayres Hall replaced beloved, but crumbling, Old College. UT Center for Educational Video and Photography

An unscheduled protest march occurred at the May Day celebration in 1920. UTK Special Collections Library

In 1933, President Franklin D. Roosevelt appointed the first board of directors for the newly-established Tennessee Valley Authority. Dr. Harcourt A. Morgan, left, resigned as president of The University of Tennessee to accept the position of agricultural expert on TVA's Board. The other directors were Arthur E. Morgan, center, chairman; and David E. Lilienthal. Tennessee Valley Authority

Under Gen. Robert R. Neyland's inspired coaching, the Tennessee Volunteers earned national football fame on Shields-Watkins field. UT Center for Educational Video and Photography

In World War II, U.S. Air Force cadets trained on The Hill. UTK Special Collections Library

The university grew by leaps and bounds after World War II, and the few existing dormitories were seriously overcrowded. As an emergency measure, "flat-tops" no longer needed at Oak Ridge were moved to The Hill, where they housed students "on the G.I. Bill."

The "temporary" flat-tops were still there in January 1961, when Negro undergraduates were officially accepted by the university. Among the first black students who entered were Theotis Robinson, Jr.; Charles Edgar Flare; and Willie Mae Gillespie. UT Center for Educational Video and Photography

During the 1960s, a gigantic westward expansion of the campus was accomplished in one fell swoop, with an urban renewal program that declared this 135-acre residential area "a potential slum." Photograph by Ernest B. Robertson, Jr.

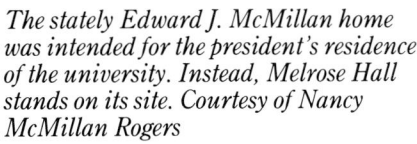

The stately Edward J. McMillan home was intended for the president's residence of the university. Instead, Melrose Hall stands on its site. Courtesy of Nancy McMillan Rogers

The W. K. McClure residence at 949 Temple Avenue was one of several handsome homes on the site of the McClung Tower. Courtesy of Robert L. McClure

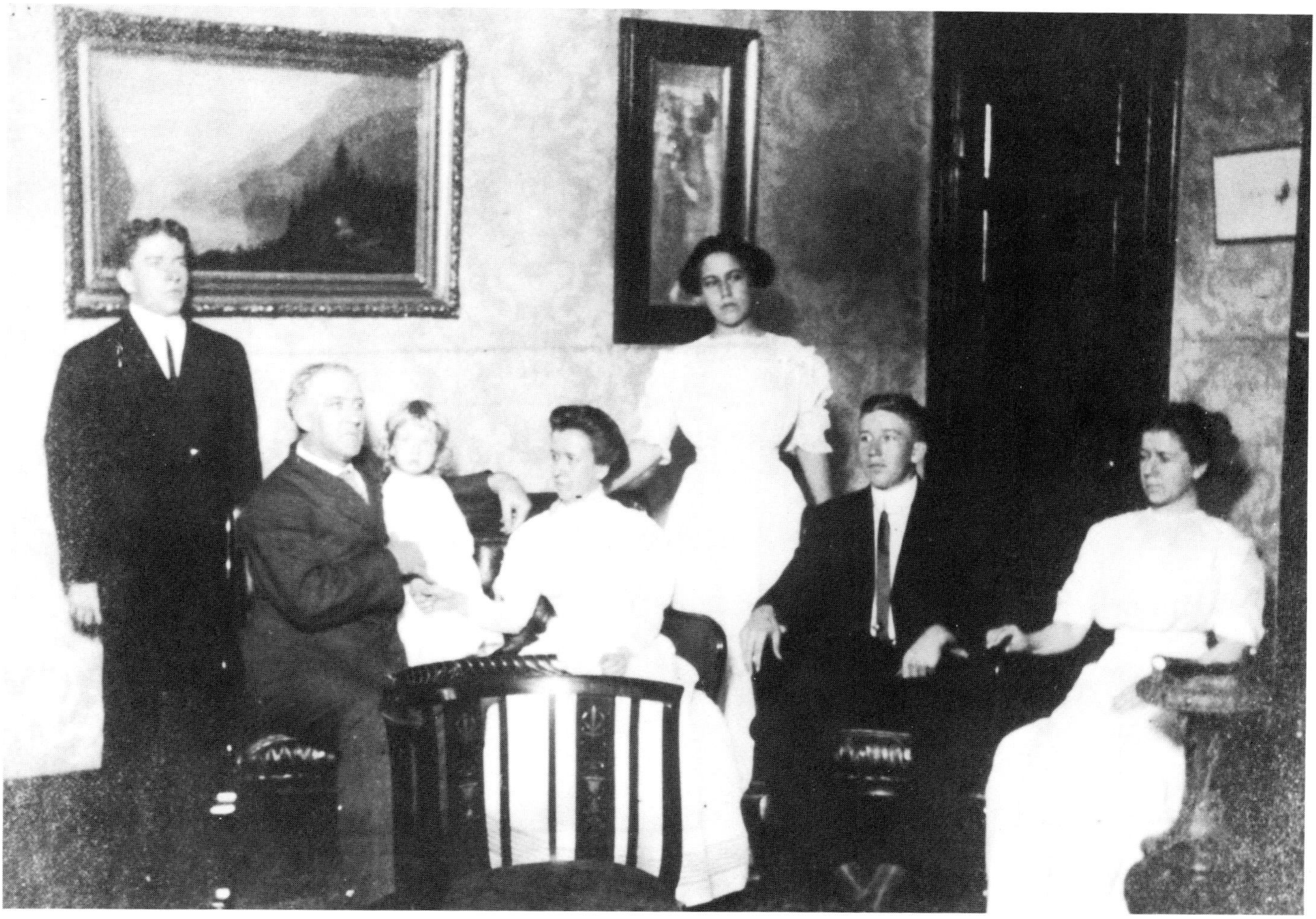

The W.K. McClure family in the parlor, circa 1910. Left to right: Wallace, Mr. and Mrs. McClure with Robert, Marguerite (Keeling), William Kyle, Jr., and Mrs. McClure's sister, Miss Sara Lewis. Courtesy of Robert L. McClure

Tree-shaded Circle Park, deeded to the city of West Knoxville in 1888, was ringed by handsome residences. The elongated structure that now follows this curve is actually two buildings: the Student Services Building; and the Communications and University Extension Building. Courtesy of C. Milton Hinshilwood

For generations of UT students, E&E was an institution at the foot of The Hill. Its Cumberland Avenue corner site was required for the lawn of the Carolyn P. Brown Memorial University Center. Courtesy of Hal Ernest

Students called the devastated area "Hiroshima West." UT Center for Educational Video and Photography

After the streets had been rearranged, the trees up-rooted and the hills downgraded, Pres. Andy Holt and Gov. Frank Clement presided over the groundbreaking ceremonies for the new Fraternity Park. UT Center for Educational Video and Photography

Twenty years later, beyond ninety-five thousand-seat Neyland Stadium's sky-boxes, the expanded campus stretches away. Nestled at the base of the stadium, at right, is Estabrook Hall, the second oldest building on The Hill. UT Center for Educational Video and Photography

"Hopecote," now the university's guesthouse on Melrose Place, was the home of Mr. and Mrs. Albert Hope. Its Knoxville-born architect, John Fanz Staub, started a national trend toward historic preservation in 1924, by building this "Cotswold cottage" around the hand-hewn beams and lintels from a barn on Adm. David Farragut's birthplace farm. The living room contains a corner cupboard from John Kain's vanished "Trafalgar" that was carved by Knox County's first architect, Thomas Hope—the great-grandfather of Hopecote's owner. Development Office, UT, Knoxville

At the end of the nineteenth century, when "Art Photography" was all the rage, this tasteful composition by Knoxville's Joseph Knaffl received worldwide acclaim. A copy of the famous "Knaffl Madonna" is prominently displayed at Hopecote because, before her marriage to Albert Hope, Miss Emma Fanz posed for the photograph holding baby Josephine Knaffl who, in later life, was Mrs. David Baker, Sr. Courtesy of Sam Knaffl, Jr.

Clarence Brown, the brilliant director of such motion picture classics as National Velvet *and* The Yearling, *was a native Knoxvillian who graduated from The University of Tennessee in 1910. Sixty years later, he returned to his alma mater for the dedication of the Clarence Brown Theatre, where he posed on stage with the stars of* The Yearling, *Jane Wyman and Claude Jarman. UTK Special Collections Library*

The John C. Hodges Library opened in 1987. The original undergraduate library is now encapsulated within the amazing ziggurat of the new state-of-the-art main library. Beginning at left in the background are: Liberal Arts' McClung Tower; the Art and Architecture Building; the Music Building; Carousel and Clarence Brown theatres; and Melrose and Hess residential halls. In the right foreground, historic Tyson House, the headquarters of the UTK Alumni Association and UTK Development Office, is encroached upon by faculty-office buildings. Photograph by Ernest B. Robertson, Jr.

Maj. Gen. Henry Knox, the Revolutionary War hero for whom Knoxville and Knox County are named, was a Boston bookseller whose hobby was the study of military tactics and ordinance. He put his theoretical knowledge to practical use, as Gen. George Washington's artillery commander. In 1789, President Washington appointed him the nation's first secretary of war. UTK Special Collections Library

Chapter 6

Knoxville— The County Seat

In 1783, when North Carolina set a bargain price on state-owned lands beyond the mountains, James White visited and purchased the future site of Knoxville. He returned in 1786, and built a comfortable two-story log house beside First Creek, a short distance from the Tennessee River; the following year, he turned his house into a fort by adding outbuildings and a protective stockade of sharpened stakes.

White was one of many settlers whose property had been deeded to them by the state of North Carolina before the U.S. government's 1785 treaty with the Cherokee gave mid-East Tennessee back to the Indians. Justifiably, the Cherokee viewed these settlers as trespassers to be driven out. Until the area became part of the Territory of the United States South of the River Ohio in 1790, corn crops were frequently burned, isolated cabins were often raided, and no solitary traveler was safe from ambush.

With his constituents' lands and lives at stake, territorial governor William Blount summoned the Cherokee to a treaty meeting at the frontier outpost of White's Fort, which was close (but not too close) to the Indian towns on the Little Tennessee River. After days of hard bargaining, the Treaty of Holston was signed on July 2, 1791, by forty-one chieftains and a jubilant Governor Blount.

Blount had succeeded in buying the Cherokees' claim to most of East Tennessee's mid-section, including all of what is now Knox County. He decided to place the nation's first territorial capital at the site of the all-important treaty meeting, and to name it for Maj. Gen. Henry Knox who, as the United States secretary of war, was responsible for its defense "against all enemies, foreign and domestic."

Blount obtained from James White a beautiful, and defensible, townsite: the same rectangular plateau bounded on the south by the Tennessee River, on the east and west by the valleys of large creeks, and on the north by a deep ravine, that is today's Downtown Knoxville. White's son-in-law, Charles McClung, took on the task of laying out a "capital city" with ten streets, sixteen square blocks, and sixty-four half-acre lots. These parcels were

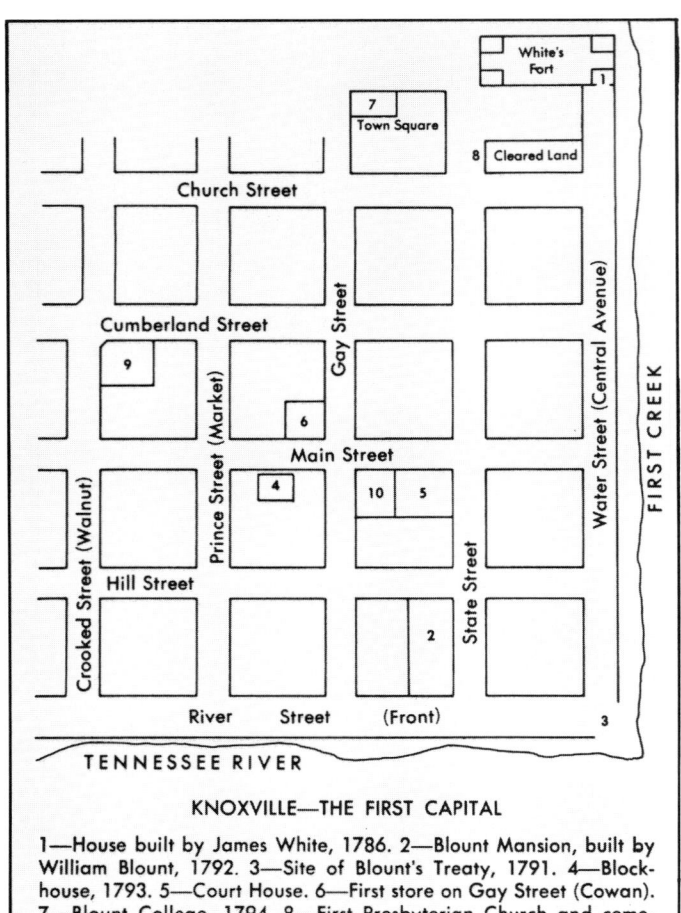

Knoxville, *by Betsey Beeler Creekmore*

assigned to purchasers by a public lottery on October 3, 1791, and this is the official date of Knoxville's founding.

Meanwhile the Cherokee, noting that the territory's seat of government was within easy striking distance of their own capital city of Chota on the Little Tennessee, were demanding—and receiving from the federal government—increased payment for their relinquished rights.

At the corner of Hill and State streets, wealthy William Blount built a governor's mansion, and a separate one-room office that was the Territory's only capitol. There, on June 11, 1792, a gubernatorial decree created Knox County and designated Knoxville as the county seat.

The two-story log house built by James White in 1786 was sold early in the nineteenth century to James Kennedy, Jr., who preserved it by adaptive use. Disguised with clapboard sheathing, it became the kitchen wing of the State Street residence shown in this photograph from the UTK Special Collections Library. The State Street Municipal Garage now occupies its site.

This is the very house erected by James White in 1786, five years before Knoxville was founded. From early in the nineteenth century until 1906, it served as the kitchen wing of a brick mansion on State Street, and has since survived two moves to remain a local landmark. Photograph by Ron Childress

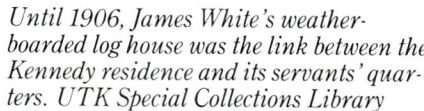

Until 1906, James White's weatherboarded log house was the link between the Kennedy residence and its servants' quarters. UTK Special Collections Library

Before the Kennedy home was torn down in 1906, the historic kitchen wing was purchased by Isaiah Ford, who removed its weatherboarding and carefully numbered the squared timbers as they were lifted down. He then reassembled Knoxville's oldest house south of the river on Woodlawn Pike.

This unique photograph from the McClung Historical Collection shows how James White's log house emerged intact when its tin roof and clapboard covering were stripped away.

William Blount was only forty-three years old when he was appointed governor of the Territory of the United States South of the River Ohio, but he had already devoted a life time to public service—as paymaster for the North Carolina militia during the Revolutionary War, as a member of the Continental Congress, as speaker of the lower house of the North Carolina legislature, and, most importantly, as a signer of the United States Constitution for his native state.

This photograph of an etching, signed "Albert Rosenthal, Phila. 1800," was provided by the McClung Historical Collection of the Knox County Public library.

Building this two-story frame house in the western wilderness was a monumental task in 1792. Every length of dressed lumber was floated down the French Broad River from North Carolina; nails and hardware came down the Holston River from Kings' Iron Works at Kingsport; and each pane of glass had to be brought by packhorse from Virginia. For its time and place, Gov. William Blount's new house was indeed a mansion! Blount Mansion Association

Louis Philippe, Duc d'Orleans, the future king of France, was royally entertained at Blount Mansion when he visited Knoxville with his two younger brothers in 1797. Photograph by Nick Myers of an etching owned by Blount Mansion Association

The famous French botanist, André Michaux, was a dinner guest at Blount Mansion in 1796. He liked this beautiful area so much that he returned in 1802. McClung Historical Collection

The Territory South of the River Ohio was the first federal territory to have an on-site government of its own, and Gov. William Blount's one-room office at Knoxville was America's first territorial capitol building. Here, on June 11, 1792, Knox County was created by a stroke of the governor's quill pen. Blount Mansion Association

Gov. William Blount's office looked like this in 1925, when "some old, dilapidated buildings" on the corner of Hill and State streets were about to be replaced by a parking garage. Miss Mary Boyce Temple secured an option on the property, and the newly formed East Tennessee Historical Society joined Bonny Kate Chapter of the DAR in raising funds to purchase and restore Governor Blount's Mansion and his office, the "Cradle of Tennessee History." UTK Special Collections Library

Blount Mansion, Knox County's only registered national historic landmark, became the area's first house museum in 1930. Five years later, this photograph of the drawing room appeared in the History of Homes and Gardens of Tennessee which was published by the Garden Study Club of Nashville.

Flanking the mantel are portraits of the territorial governor William Blount (left) and his half-brother Willie Blount, who served as Tennessee's third governor from 1809 to 1815.

John Chisholm's Tavern, built in 1792 adjoining the garden of Blount Mansion, housed many of Governor Blount's prominent guests. The original log structure was soon weatherboarded, and improved with mantels and a staircase designed by Knoxville's first professionally-trained architect, Thomas Hope. When Chisholm Tavern was razed in 1962 for the construction of Neyland Drive, its historic hand-carved woodwork was moved to nearby Craighead-Jackson House (the Visitors Center for Blount Mansion) which was then undergoing restoration.
History of Homes and Gardens of Tennessee

When James White sold the land on which Knoxville would be built, he reserved the plot of ground he had first cleared (and planted to turnips) in 1786, and gave it to the new town for church purposes. The First Presbyterian Church still occupies that site, along with its cemetery that contains the graves of James White and Gov. William Blount. The present building replaces a smaller sanctuary that served as a Civil War hospital and as headquarters of the Freedmens' Bureau. Greater Knoxville Chamber of Commerce

In 1792, the Cherokee of the Lower Towns formally declared war on the United States. To protect Knoxville, the territorial capital, the U.S. Army built and garrisoned a large blockhouse fort where the Old Knox County Courthouse now stands. The fort served its purpose on September 25, 1793, when the boom of its sunrise cannon averted an imminent attack by several hundred Cherokee and Creek warriors.

The Old Courthouse was new in 1884. When it opened on the Blockhouse site, this painting by Knoxville artist Lloyd Branson filled one wall of the entrance hall. It now hangs in the Tennessee State Museum at Nashville. Photograph, circa 1885, from the Author's Collection

In 1796, fifty-five delegates to the constitutional convention for the new state of Tennessee met in the large office of David Henley, U.S. Army agent, for whom Henley Street and Bridge are named. This tabletop model of the office shows formally dressed William Blount who presided at the convention, and soberly clad Charles McClung who drafted the constitution, welcoming a delegate wearing fringed buckskin and a coonskin cap. The American Flag in the corner has fifteen stars (and fifteen stripes): Tennessee was about to become the sixteenth state.

The miniature room is displayed at Blount Mansion, as is David Henley's desk on which the state constitution was signed. Photograph by Nick Myers

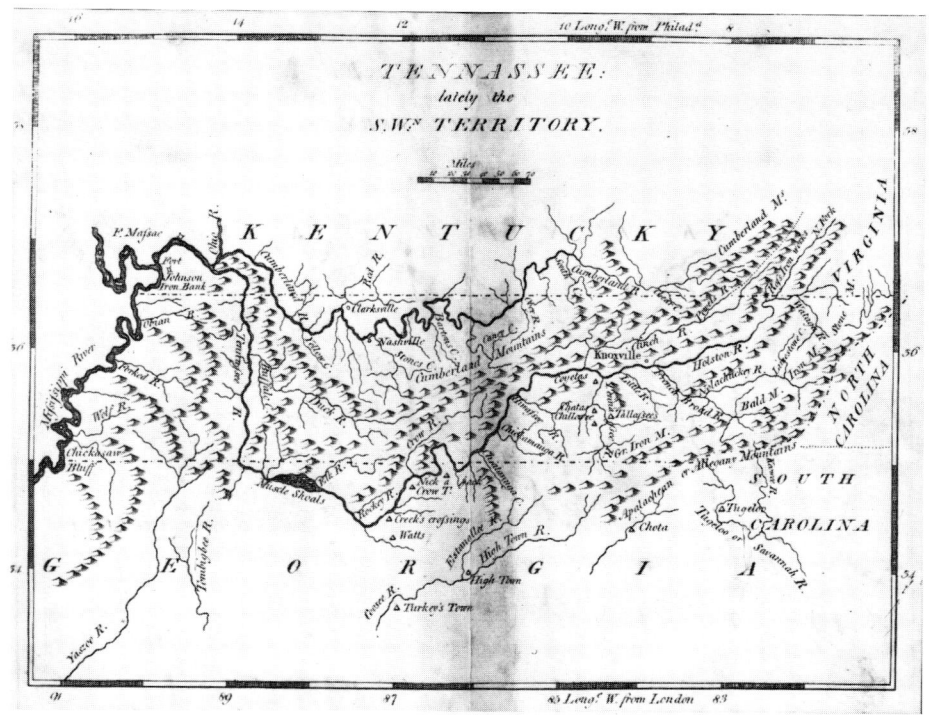

When the Territory South of the River Ohio was admitted to the Federal Union on June 1, 1796, Knoxville relinquished the title of territorial capital to become the first capital of the state of Tennessee.

John Sevier had been a military hero before becoming the first governor of the sixteenth state. He chose to wear the uniform of a major general in the territorial militia when he sat for this portrait by Charles Willson Peale that is displayed in Tennessee's capitol. McClung Historical Collection

Although Knoxville was Tennessee's seat of government for fifteen years, no capitol building was erected here. Instead, Gov. John Sevier rented this commodious dwelling from Charles McClung in 1797, and used it as a town house for his family as well as for transacting the business of the state. It continued to stand at the corner of Cumberland and Central until the 1920s. Author's Collection

Walnut Street makes a distinct jog as it crosses Cumberland Avenue, because the foundations for Gov. John Sevier's elegant townhouse were already in place when the street was widened and extended. The house, unfinished at the time of Sevier's death in 1815, was for more than a century the home of the prominent Park family.

The front porch was a late-nineteenth century addition. It was removed when the beautifully restored Sevier-Park House became the headquarters of the Knox County Academy of Medicine. Homes and Gardens of Tennessee

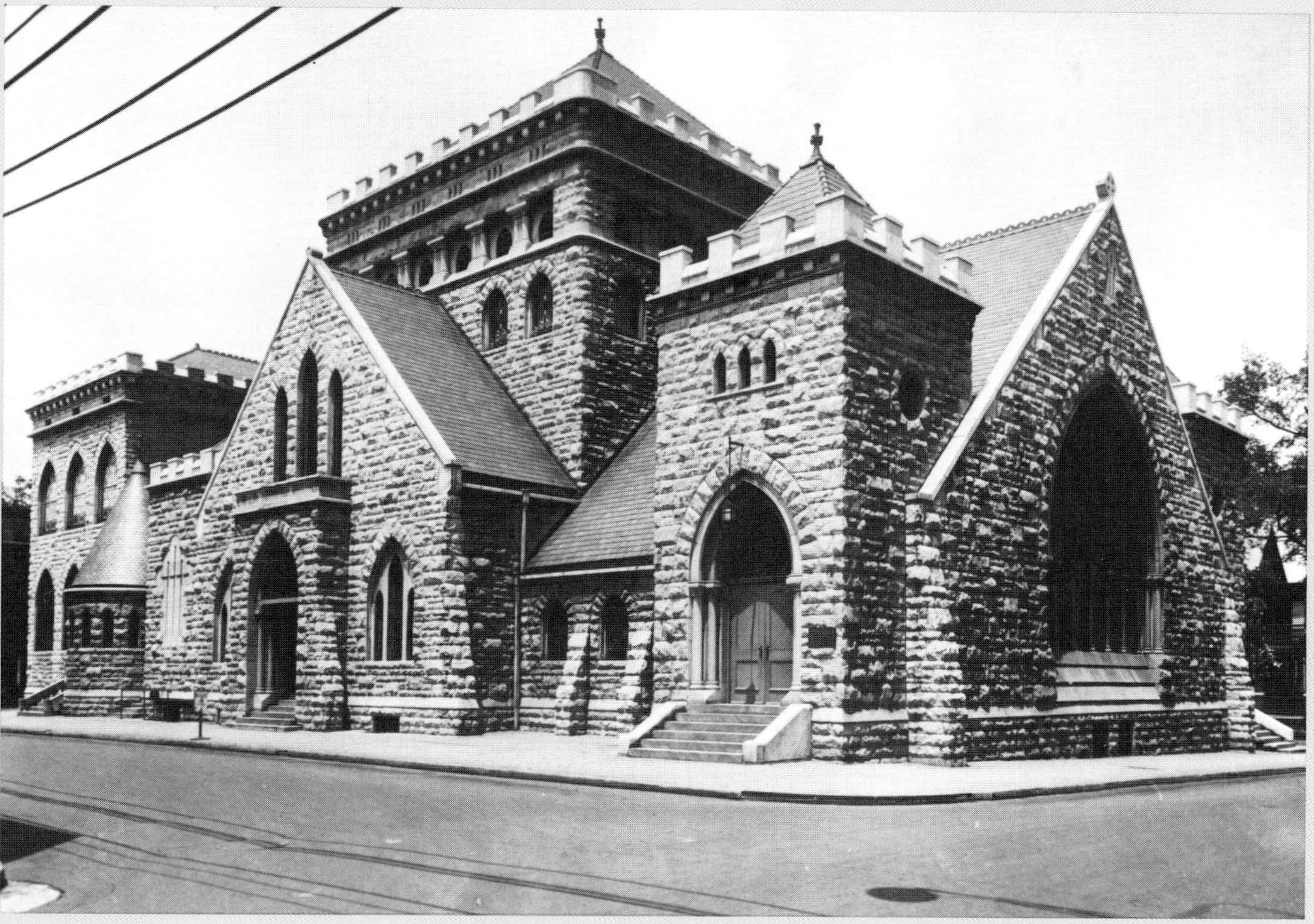

St. John's Episcopal Church has occupied the opposite corner of Cumberland and Walnut streets since 1845. The present sanctuary, built in 1893, became St. John's Cathedral in 1986. McClung Historical Collection

As the Civil War approached, Knox Countians' sentiments were sharply divided: in Knoxville, secession was supported, but the rest of the county strongly favored preservation of the Federal Union. As the war progressed, Knox County became a battleground where opposing armies fought for control of the East Tennessee, Virginia, and Georgia Railroad—the only link between the Confederate capital at Richmond and the Gulf States.

Knoxville was held by the Confederacy in the early years of the Civil War. This rare photograph shows the Stars and Bars flying above the roof of the Tennessee School for the Deaf (built in 1848) which served as a military hospital. McClung Historical Collection

The Unionists' chief spokesman was a Methodist minister, William Gannaway Brownlow, who owned and edited the bitterly biased Knoxville Whig. *In 1861, while Knoxville was held by the Confederacy, Parson Brownlow was arrested and jailed; he was later exiled with his family to the North.* Parson Brownlow's Book

Gen. Ambrose Burnside is better known for his whiskers than for his military exploits, but when he marched on Knoxville with several thousand Union troops in 1863, the small Confederate garrison vacated the city without a struggle. Courtesy of David D. Creekmore

In the 1850s, Knoxville's first professional dentist, Dr. John Fouché, rented a building that still stands at the corner of Gay and Clinch streets. After the Union Army marched into the city in 1863, Dr. Fouché bought the property from its angry owner, a Southern sympathizer who demanded payment in Confederate money! Courtesy of Isabel Ashe Bonnyman, a Fouché descendant, for whom Knoxville artist Russell Briscoe painted the building as it appeared in the 1870s. Photograph by Gary Heatherly

Gen. Orlando M. Poe and his U.S. Army engineers took advantage of the natural features of the townsite in planning Knoxville's defenses against an expected Confederate counter-attack that was not long in coming. Moats were created by damming First and Second creeks. Cannon batteries were mounted on Summit Hill overlooking the all-important railroad tracks, on College Hill commanding the western approach by way of Kingston Pike, and on Fort Hill above the road leading eastward toward Virginia.

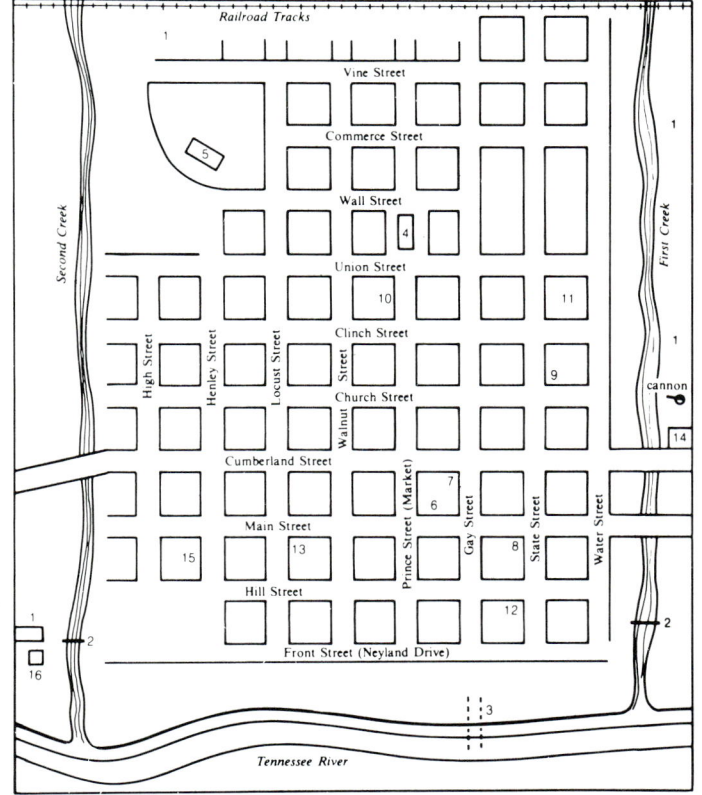

Legend:
1-Artillery batteries;
2-Dams that flooded First and Second Creeks; 3-Pontoon bridge and "Great Chain" across the Tennessee River;
4-The Market House-powder magazine;
5-School for the Deaf;* 6-Knox County Courthouse;
7-Lamar House Hotel;* 8-Bell House Hotel;* 9-First Presbyterian Church;*
10-Second Presbyterian Church;*
11-James White's house;* 12-Blount Mansion; 13-Perez Dickinson's house;
14-Parson Brownlow's house; 15-East Tennessee Female Institute;* 16-East Tennessee University.*
* commandeered for hospitals
Knoxville, *by Betsey Beeler Creekmore*

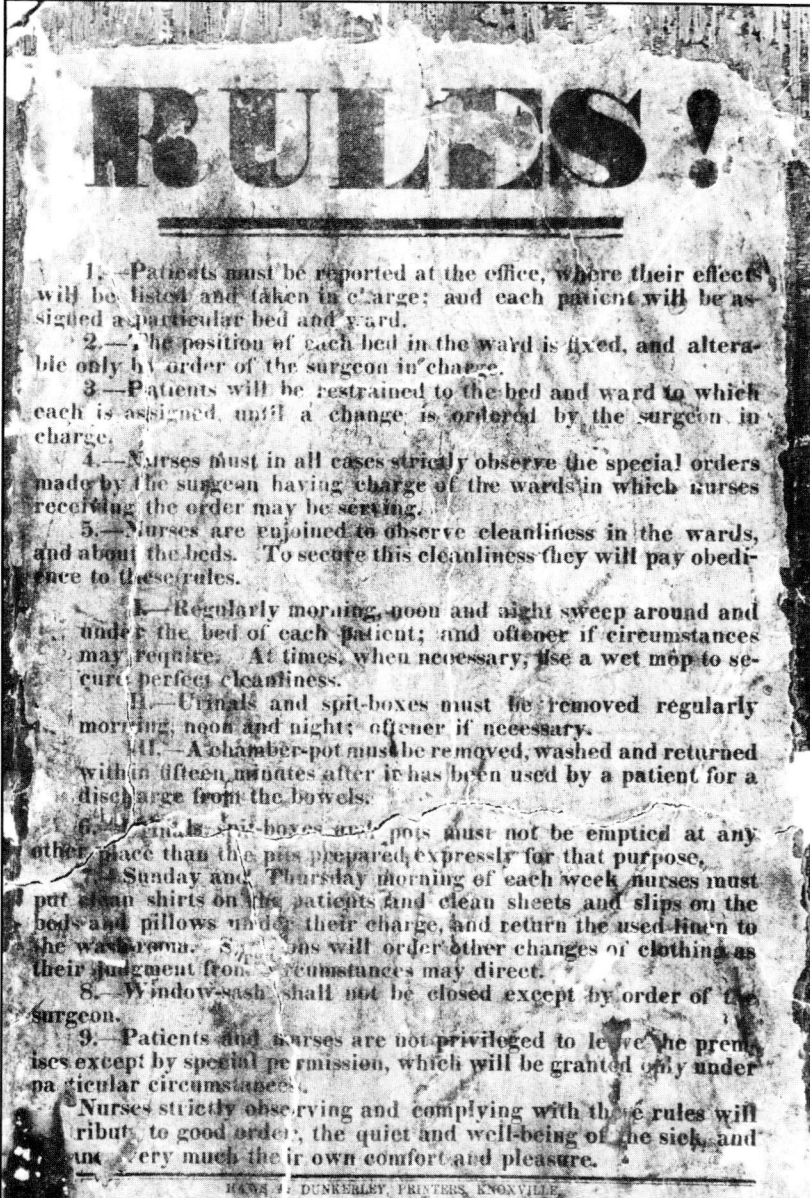

In November 1863, Gen. James Longstreet's Confederate forces surrounded the fortified city and laid siege to it.

At this time, the School for the Deaf became a U.S. Army hospital, and regulations for patient care were posted on the walls of every ward. Those rules are still legible on this fragment of plaster found in the 1920s when the building was renovated for use as Knoxville's City Hall. UTK Center for the Study of War and Society

While General W.T. Sherman's army was quick-marching to the relief of the city, the Confederate siege was lifted overnight. Knoxville remained in Union hands, and Parson Brownlow returned rejoicing to resume publication of the Whig.

This drawing, from the April 9, 1864 issue of Harper's Weekly, *shows the Brownlows arriving by U.S. Military Transport, i.e., in a freight car.*

After the war (at a time when former Confederates were denied the right to vote), William G. Brownlow was elected Tennessee's Reconstruction governor and subsequently served in the United States Senate. He was still a controversial figure in 1987, when the legislature voted to remove his portrait from the state capitol. UPI photograph, the Knoxville News-Sentinel

Father Abram Joseph Ryan, the "Poet-Priest of the Confederacy," was in charge of Knoxville's tiny Roman Catholic Mission on Summit Hill when he wrote his masterpiece, "The Conquered Banner," on a brown peanut-bag—the only paper available in the shortage-beset city. Twenty years later, in 1884, the present Church of the Immaculate Conception was built on west Vine Avenue with a large parochial school beside it. McClung Historical Collection

Market Square was given to the city of Knoxville in 1853 by William G. Swan and Joseph A. Mabry, Jr., on condition that it always remain a public market place. This contract has been breached only once, in 1863, when the one-story shed-like market house shown at left was commandeered by the United States Army for a powder magazine. Courtesy of Ernest Tracy

Peter Kern's Bakery and Confectionery, at the corner of Market Square and Union Avenue, was Knoxville's meeting place in the Gay Nineties. Above the first floor ice cream parlor was a ballroom, presided over by a French dancing master, where young ladies and gentlemen waltzed to the strains of a gilded harp. Commercial History of Tennesee

The main entrance to the new two-story market house was this imposing structure built in 1897 at the south end of Market Square. The City Hall at the north end of the Square also contained the central fire station. Commercial History of Tennessee

In 1900, the Knoxville Chamber of Commerce met at the Public Hall on the second floor of the Market House. Seated on the platform, facing the camera, is the Chamber's president, A.J. Albers. UTK Special Collections Library

Everybody came to the Market House to shop! On a snowy morning during World War I, Mrs. Alfred Sanford (Eleanor Spence) and Mrs. N. E. ("Whittie") Logan brought the obligatory market baskets of white oak splits.

Experts believe the custom-built limousine was a Renault, with an air-cooled engine that was started by cranking and had no neutral gear. Therefore, the uniformed chauffeur remained behind the wheel, with one foot on the clutch and the other on the brake, to keep the engine running and the car stationary while his passengers descended. McClung Historical Collection

Homegrown vegetables and fruits in season were sold along both sides of Market Square. McClung Historical Collection

183

Permanent stalls inside the Market House specialized in bakery products, fresh meats, staples, and "shipped" produce. Country butter and homemade cottage cheese were sold from tables in the center of the floor. McClung Historical Collection

When the beloved but antiquated Market House burned in 1960, Market Square became a pedestrian mall where cast-concrete umbrellas sheltered the sidewalks and formed a small marketing facility that satisfied the deed of gift. Photograph by Bill Tracy

A 1985 renovation of Market Square returned it to the character of a nineteenth century "village." Bright awnings replaced the cement sidewalk shelters of the mall, and permanent staging was provided for such temporary attractions as the ice-skating rink, a highlight of Christmas in the City. Courtesy of Knoxville/Knox County Tennessee Homecoming '86 Committee

After the Civil War, Knoxville became the hub of rail transportation for a several-state area, and the wholesale distribution center for the entire upper south. Warehouses with track-side loading docks were unloaded on Jackson Avenue, where this area at the corner of Central Avenue is now undergoing restoration. McClung Historical Collection

In April 1897, the east side of Gay Street between Commerce and Union avenues was destroyed by a fire that burned for days, feeding on the contents of eight huge wholesale houses. Alerted by telegraph, the Chattanooga Fire Department loaded men and equipment on railroad flatcars, and highballed to the aid of Knoxville's embattled fire fighters. McClung Historical Collection

The combined fire departments managed to confine the flames to the north side of Union Avenue, so the Cowan McClung and Company's 1873 building was spared. Remodeled in the 1920s by Fidelity Bankers Trust Company, it still graces the corner of Gay and Union. Courtesy of Mary Thomas Fleury

Within a year, the buildings leveled by fire were replaced and their tenants re-installed. W. W. Woodruff & Company, Gay Street's oldest business, still occupies its restored structure, in the center of this photograph by Rob Childress.

Before the turn of the century, Knoxville's first department store opened in one of the rebuilt structures. The M.M. Newcomer Company filled all five floors of the former jobbing house, and Newcomer's Pharmacy occupied the tiny adjoining building. This photograph was made in 1910 for the Commercial History of Tennessee, *published by the Travelers' Protective Association.*

In the 1950s, property owners connected their buildings on Gay Street's east side, from Union to Wall avenues, with a covered Promenade at the rear and added a moving staircase from the parking lot on State Street. This experimental outdoor escalator worked for a brief time only. Photograph by Bill Tracy

In 1962, the sidewalks on both sides of Gay Street between Clinch and Wall avenues were covered with metal canopies to protect pedestrians from sun and rain. Bill Tracy's photograph shows the crowd looking forward to a Shrine parade.

Fashions change—in urban design as well as in clothing. In 1985, when Knoxville was chosen to participate in the Main Street program of the National Trust for Historic Preservation, removing the Gay/Way canopies was the first priority in Main Street, Knoxville's revitalization effort.

We love a parade!

The judging stand in front of the Fouché building, during a parade of fine livestock on Gay Street in 1873. Moments after this photograph was taken, Col. Perez Dickinson's prize-winning thousand-pound hog lay down on his bulging side nearby, and died! Author's Collection

The theme song for a Fourth of July parade in the 1880s must have been "Roll Out the Barrel." Author's Collection

A late 1880s circus parade edging past horse-drawn streetcars in the five hundred block of Gay Street. McClung Historical Collection

Off to the Spanish-American War! Knox County's own regiment, the Sixth U.S. Volunteers, was commanded by Col. Lawrence D. Tyson, with Cary F. Spence as regimental adjutant and Horace Van Deventer as quartermaster. McClung Historical Collection

UT cadets joined the victory celebration in 1899. The flag of the city of Knoxville hangs from the balcony at right, below the sign of McCrary and Branson Photo Studio, where Lloyd Branson designed the city's official emblem in 1896, for the Tennessee Centennial. McClung Historical Collection

...And we won't come back
'Til it's over, Over There!

This photograph of the Third Tennessee Infantry's departure on September 7, 1917, is from Knox County in the World War, *published by the Knoxville Lithographing Company in 1919.*

The ladies of Knoxville welcomed the 117th Infantry home in 1919 with a seated luncheon. A double row of tables filled Walnut Street from Cumberland Avenue to Church Street, and the feast was prepared in the kitchens of two churches, St. John's Episcopal, right, and Second Presbyterian, left, whose site is now occupied by Lawson McGhee Library. Knox County in the World War

The Halls Community's float was the grand prize winner in the 1958 Santa Claus Parade. The carolers on the "Christmas Showboat" were members of the Halls High School Chorus. Knoxville News-Sentinel

Each April, scores of marching bands open the seventeen-day Dogwood Arts Festival that celebrates Knoxville's breathtaking beauty with more than three hundred events, made possible by eight thousand volunteers. Greater Knoxville Chamber of Commerce

Southern Railway Depot, Knoxville, Tenn.

Since 1854, there have been railroad tracks in the deep ravine at the north end of the downtown plateau. In 1904, access to the new Southern Railway Station was provided by a driveway for carriages, hacks, and Railway Express wagons—plus a pedestrian walkway from Depot Street that ended on the station's second floor. Courtesy of C. Milton Hinshilwood

Day or night, whenever a World War I troop train stopped at the Southern Station, the Red Cross Canteen was ready with free coffee, doughnuts, sandwiches, cigarettes, and postcards. Author's Collection

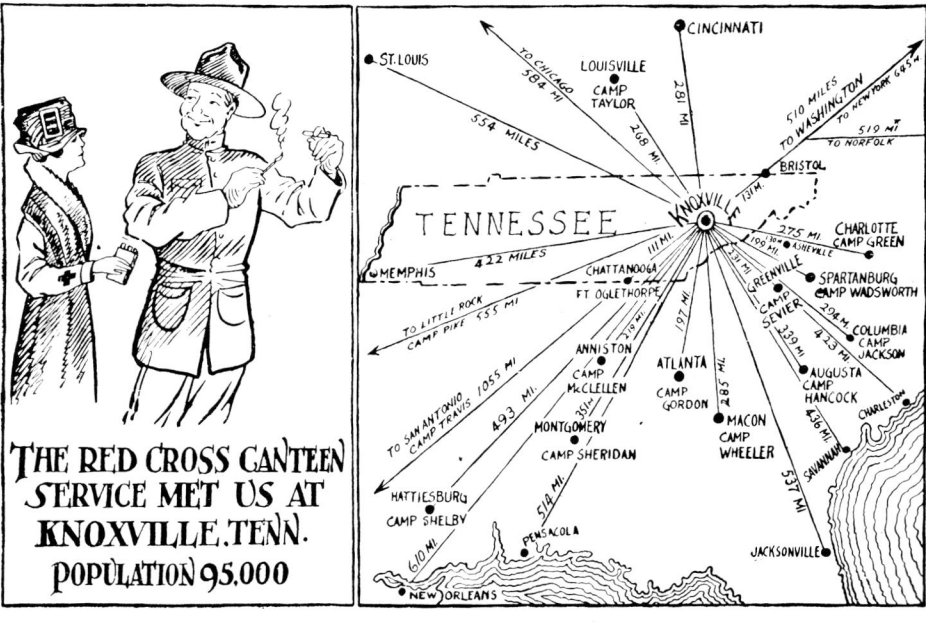

194

When the north end of Gay Street was raised fifteen feet in 1919, during the construction of a new viaduct over the Southern Railroad tracks, these one-story buildings went underground. They are still there, beneath the present structures. Knoxville News-Sentinel

From 1904 until passenger service was discontinued in 1970, overnight pullman service to Washington and New York was provided from the Southern Railway Station. McClung Historical Collection

In 1908, as this postcard testifies, Knoxville's tallest building stood at the southeast corner of Gay and Clinch streets on the original site of Blount College. It was later purchased, and more than doubled in size, by C. B. Atkin, who renamed it in honor of his wife, Mary Burwell. Author's Collection

In 1928, an elaborate moving-picture palace opened in the newer section of the Burwell Building. The Tennessee Theatre has been the scene of six world premiere performances, including So This Is Love, *based on the life of Tennessee-born opera star, Grace Moore. McClung Historical Collection*

Movies are still shown in the ornate, Spanish-moorish theatre, where a giant Wurlitzer organ rises majestically from the orchestra pit. The Tennessee also serves as the showcase for the Knoxville Symphony Orchestra and the Knoxville Opera Company. *McClung Historical Collection*

The Farragut Hotel was built on the northeast corner of Gay and Clinch in 1920, and named for a native Knox Countian. The rank of admiral in the United States Navy was especially created for David Glasgow Farragut, the hero of the Battle of Mobile Bay, whose portrait is shown above the Hotel's registration desk. Converted to offices in the 1970s, the Farragut Building houses the Knoxville headquarters of First Tennessee Bank. *McClung Historical Collection*

On their way to the inauguration of Pres. Brown Ayres at Staub's Theatre in 1905, The University of Tennessee's Corps of Cadets paraded past the Woman's Building.

This same structure had been the Knoxville Building at the Tennessee Centennial of 1897. Afterward, several Knox County women's organizations joined forces to have the building moved from the Nashville exposition grounds to Knoxville's Main Street, where it burned in 1907. UTK Special Collections Library

Mrs. Lawrence D. Tyson (Bettie McGhee) headed the Woman's Building Board that raised funds for the move by publishing the Knoxville Cookbook *in 1900.* Some Representative Women of Tennessee.

Inside a gigantic World War II quonset hut? No, the civic auditorium that replaced the Woman's Building at the corner of Main and Gay streets, decorated for the visit of a national hero, Theodore Roosevelt, to the 1910 Appalachian Exhibition. McClung Historical Collection

By the 1920s, when every section of the city was served by electric trolleys and all tracks led to Gay Street, the auditorium had been converted into a streetcar barn.
   The site, subsequently a bus terminal and parking lot, is part of the Whittle Communications redevelopment. McClung Historical Collection

Still standing at the corner of Gay and Cumberland is the "large and elegant building of three storys and fifteen rooms" that became the city's best hotel in 1817, and is now known as the Lamar House. Quite by accident, the building acquired a fourth floor in 1854, when Gay Street's surface was lowered some twelve feet in preparation for paving. Afterward, the hotel's former basement opened on the sidewalk, and a balcony was added outside the original front door. This 1877 photograph from the McClung Historical Collection shows President Rutherford B. Hayes speaking from the garlanded balcony.

In 1909 the elegant Bijou Theatre was built onto the rear of the Lamar House; the hotel's front door on Gay Street became the theatre entrance, and the sidewalk-spanning balcony was turned into a marquee. This photograph, from the McClung Historical Collection, shows the theatre's opening night audience.

Before 1920, a policeman controlling traffic at the corner of Church and Gay streets had plenty of time to answer questions. The stop-sign, mounted like a golf flag in a cup, was manually turned with a small handle on one side. In 1926, the Knoxville Sentinel *merged with the* Knoxville News *to form today's morning newspaper. UTK Special Collections Library*

In 1927, traffic at the corner of Market and Union was controlled from a signal tower in the middle of the intersection. A policeman inside the tower switched the stop *and* go *lights off and on.*

From 1905 to 1928, the Arnstein Building housed a large and elegant department store owned by erudite Max B. Arnstein, who left Germany at age sixteen, and lived for several years with his Baruch cousins at Hobcaw Plantation in South Carolina before coming to Knoxville in 1888. Mrs. Arnstein (Lalla Block) was the first woman elected to the Knox County Court. Through their generosity, the Arnstein Jewish Community Center, now located on Deane Hill Drive, was established in 1929. McClung Historical Collection

Todd & Armistead Drugstore was a long-time landmark at the southwest corner of Clinch and Market streets. About 1930, Eugene Armistead, at left, and James C. Todd at right behind the counters, reached an important milestone when Todd & Armistead filled its one millionth prescription. Thereafter, the drugstore's slogan was: "Trusted a million times." Courtesy of John M. Armistead

Lunchtime in 1939 at the S&W Cafeteria, Downtown Knoxville's all-time favorite restaurant, where soft music was provided by an organ at the front of the sweeping stairway to the balcony. Rejuvenation of the elegant art-deco building began in 1988, when it became the downtown health and fitness center of East Tennessee Baptist Hospital. McClung Historical Collection

"Country music" was born in Knoxville, where such all-time greats as Roy Acuff, Chet Atkins, and Archie Campbell first starred on the WNOX Tennessee Barn Dance. Fans lined up outside the station's Gay Street studio in 1949, to see and hear the live radio broadcast. Knoxville News-Sentinel

"Signs of the times." The large department store built between Henley and Locust streets by Rich's of Atlanta in 1954 has subsequently been marked "Miller's" and "Hess's." Knoxville News-Sentinel

Knoxville's reward for withstanding a Civil War Confederate siege was a new U.S. Post Office and Customs House, built of locally-quarried white marble, that appears at the left in this early photograph of Clinch Street, looking west from Gay. McClung Historical Collection

After its establishment in 1933, the Tennessee Valley Authority was headquarted in Knoxville's Customs House for forty years. Restoring the vacated building as the repository of city and county archives dating back to territorial days was the first project approved by the Bicentennial Commission of Knoxville and Knox County. Now the East Tennessee Historical Center, it also houses the nationally-important McClung Historical Collection.

This photograph shows the structure's south side, which is hidden behind the Center Square Towers. Knoxville Convention and Visitors Bureau

Native Knoxvillian Charles E. Krutch was the brother of a noted author, Joseph Wood Krutch, and a nephew of the nineteenth century landscape artist, Charles Christopher Krutch. As TVA's chief photographer, he left a record of regional history that is known within the Authority as the K-File. Tennessee Valley Authority

His bequest of 1½ million dollars to the city of Knoxville made possible the establishment of Krutch Park, a green oasis on downtown Market Street in the block north of the Customs House. City of Knoxville Information Office

After forty years of renting scattered office space, the Tennessee Valley Authority built a home of its own. Two blocks of Market Street were closed in the early 1970s, in order to locate the fraternal-twin TVA towers at the north end of Market Square. Knoxville Convention and Visitors Bureau

When Summit Hill Drive was created for better access to TVA's headquarters, two well-loved landmarks fell before the bulldozers. One was the Commerce Avenue Fire Hall, shown in this turn-of-the-century photograph. The first downtown YMCA appears at right. Courtesy of the late Ralph Diggs

Knoxville Heritage, Inc., was formed in protest against the overnight destruction of Old Lawson-McGhee Library, built of Tennessee marble in 1916, on Summit Hill. Many groups, including the Nicholson Art League, found the library a convenient meeting place. McClung Historical Collection

This is the lady for whom Knox County's Lawson McGhee Library is named. After the untimely death of May Lawson McGhee (Williams) at the age of twenty-three, a public library was established in her memory by her father, Col. Charles McGhee, in 1885. McClung Historical Collection

The C. J. McClung family and staff posed at their elegant new residence on Main Street in 1875. President and Mrs. Grover Cleveland were house guests here in the 1890s. Courtesy of Mary Thomas Fleury

On Main Street, in the 1920s, the graceful spire of the First Baptist Church succeeded the minarets of the McClung house. Knox County's largest congregation filled the sanctuary that is reminiscent of London's St. Martin's-in-the-Fields. McClung Historical Collection

All Knoxville mourned the passing of this century-old Main Street landmark, torn down for a parking lot. Built in the 1840s by prominent Perez Dickinson, it was purchased in 1904 by equally prominent C. B. Atkin, who added the semi-circular portico. McClung Historical Collection.

On August 10, 1905, Mrs. C. B. Atkin gave a birthday party for her eldest daughter Edith (Mrs. Ned Lutz). The honoree is seated in the center of the second row, with her sister Eleanor (Mrs. Kennedy Craig) on her right. Little sister Marian (Mrs. Charles Rankin) is at their feet. Anne Henegar (Mrs. Matt Thomas), seated at right front, kindly provided the picture.

Until 1933, when their block was cleared for a new Post Office, the McTeer, Lewis, Ault, and Nash residences stood on the north side of Main Street. Visible in the background of this photograph from the McClung Historical Collection is the recently completed Medical Arts Building.

The Lyceum, at the southwest corner of Walnut and Cumberland, also was demolished to make way for the Post Office. The gray stucco house and its auditorium-annex were jointly owned by four women's organizations: Ossoli Circle; Bonny Kate Chapter of the DAR; Chapter 89 of the UDC; and the Tuesday Morning Music Club. Senior citizens recall that Miss Annie McGhee's dancing classes were held here, and that piano lessons were given by Prof. Frank Nelson in an upstairs studio. McClung Historical Collection

The Main Post Office, completed in 1934, was "demoted" in 1986 to the Downtown Post Office. Its exterior of locally-quarried marble looks white in sunny weather but turns rose pink on rainy days. Author's Collection

"Maplehurst," high above the river at the western end of Hill Street, was the home of Edward Terry Sanford, Knox County's only justice of the United States Supreme Court (1923-1930). The house burned after it was sold by Justice Sanford, but a residential enclave on its grounds retains the Maplehurst name. Robert R. VanDeventer Collection, in the McClung Historical Collection

Still to be found at 615 West Hill Avenue is the house built early in this century by A. Percy Lockett to remind his bride of her Mississippi home. Formerly the First Church of Christ, Scientist, it is easily identified now as the Lord Lindsay restaurant. McClung Historical Collection

Prestigious pedal-cars on Hill Street in the 1920s: Mary Frances Dickey's Oakland, left, and Howard Lumsden's Packard. The truck in the background was delivering "fancy groceries" from T. E. Burns & Company. Courtesy of Howard Lumsden

Unlikely though it seems, the Church Street United Methodist Church stands on Henley Street, between Main and Hill avenues. The church moved to this location in 1931, after its Church Street sanctuary was destroyed by fire. Photograph by Ernest B. Robertson, Jr.

Blount College ceased to admit female students when it became East Tennessee College and moved from Gay Street to The Hill, but higher education for women did not end. The East Tennessee Female Institute opened in 1828, in this building facing Main Street on the site of the Church Street United Methodist Church, and continued in operation until women were readmitted to The University of Tennessee in 1893. Beginning in 1850, the institute conferred upon its graduates the degree of "Mistress of Polite Literature"! Author's Collection

In 1884, Knox County's government moved across Main Street to an imposing Queen Anne style courthouse built on the site of the early Blockhouse Fort. In this 1905 photograph from the UTK Special Collections Library, cannon flank the front steps, and a double horse trough at curbside supports the statue of a fireman with a baby in his arms.

In the 1920s, the Fireman's Statue was moved from the Courthouse to the lawn of Old City Hall where this closeup, provided by the UT Center for Educational Video and Photography, was made. It now stands in front of the Knoxville Fire Department's headquarters on Summit Hill Drive.

The statue, paid for by public subscription, is a memorial to William F. (Tump) Maxey and John J. Dunn. The two firemen were killed on February 2, 1904, in the collapse of the blazing M. L. Ross Wholesale Grocery building on Gay Street.

In 1815 John Sevier, who had served six terms as governor and two terms in the U.S. House of Representatives, was sent by President James Monroe to locate and mark the boundary line agreed upon at the end of the Creek War. While on this mission, he died suddenly of a fever and was buried near Fort Decatur, Alabama.

In 1897, the body of Tennessee's first governor was brought home from its Alabama resting place and ceremonially reinterred on the Courthouse lawn in Knoxville, Tennessee's first capital. John Sevier's two wives, Sarah Hawkins and Catherine Sherrill (Bonny Kate), were later reburied here, one on either side of the governor's grave. Author's Collection

Until 1925, the Ward, Beeler, Cunningham, Knaffl, and Hurst homes faced the courthouse across South Gay Street. They were razed for the construction of the Tennessee Terrace Hotel. Author's Collection

The hotel building stood unfinished for two years, after its developers went into bankruptcy. McClung Historical Collection

Refinanced and re-named, the Hotel Andrew Johnson opened in December 1929; it prospered during the Depression years, because its elegant appointments and superior services attracted 130 resident guests. Renovated for offices, it is now the Andrew Johnson Plaza. McClung Historical Collection

Learning's portal, for children born within the sound of the Courthouse clock, was this doorway at The Bell House. Built at the corner of Main and State streets in the 1850s as a hotel, it served as a Civil War hospital; in 1872 it became the first city-owned public school. It was razed for the construction of a new City and County Bank Building. Knoxville News-Sentinel

History repeats itself. The Riverview Towers stood first unfinished and then unoccupied for years, after the 1983 failure of the Butcher-owned City and County banks. It now has come to life as the headquarters of the Bank Of East Tennessee. Photograph by Gary Heatherly

This 1869 photograph from the McClung Historical Collection shows Gay Street looking north from the Main Street corner. The first and second buildings at right were occupied by the Elgin Drugstore and the Colonial Hotel in 1962, when the block was purchased by Millers Department Store and cleared for a new building that never materialized.

Staub's Opera House, on the southeast corner of Gay and Cumberland, celebrated its grand opening in 1872 with a performance of William Tell. In 1920, it became part of the Lowe's Vaudeville Circuit; in the 1940s, as the Lyric Theatre, it was the scene of professional wrestling matches. Miller's parking lot replaced the theatre, and the Colonial Hotel next door. McClung Historical Collection

On the parking lot bounded by Gay, Main, State, and Cumberland, the spectacular headquarters of the United American bank was completed in time for the 1982 World's Fair. Following the UAB's spectacular failure in 1983, the sky-blue glass structure was renamed Plaza Tower. Knoxville Convention and Visitors Bureau

Two blocks of Market Street, between Main Avenue and Neyland Drive, were closed by the construction of joint governmental headquarters for Knoxville and Knox County, in the shadow of the now-restored Old Courthouse. Before the City/County Building officially opened in 1980, it hosted an impressive "Sports Exhibition" from Soviet Russia. Public Building Authority of Knox County

From 1925 to 1980, the antebellum campus of the School for the Deaf was Knoxville's City Hall, and an effort was made to unify the mismatched brick buildings by painting them white. (In early days, TSD's former classrooms were occupied by Boyd Junior High School.) After the completion of the City/County Building in 1980, painstaking restoration returned this vacated complex to its original appearance. Since 1983, it has housed supplementary TVA offices. Photograph by Ron Childress, 1976

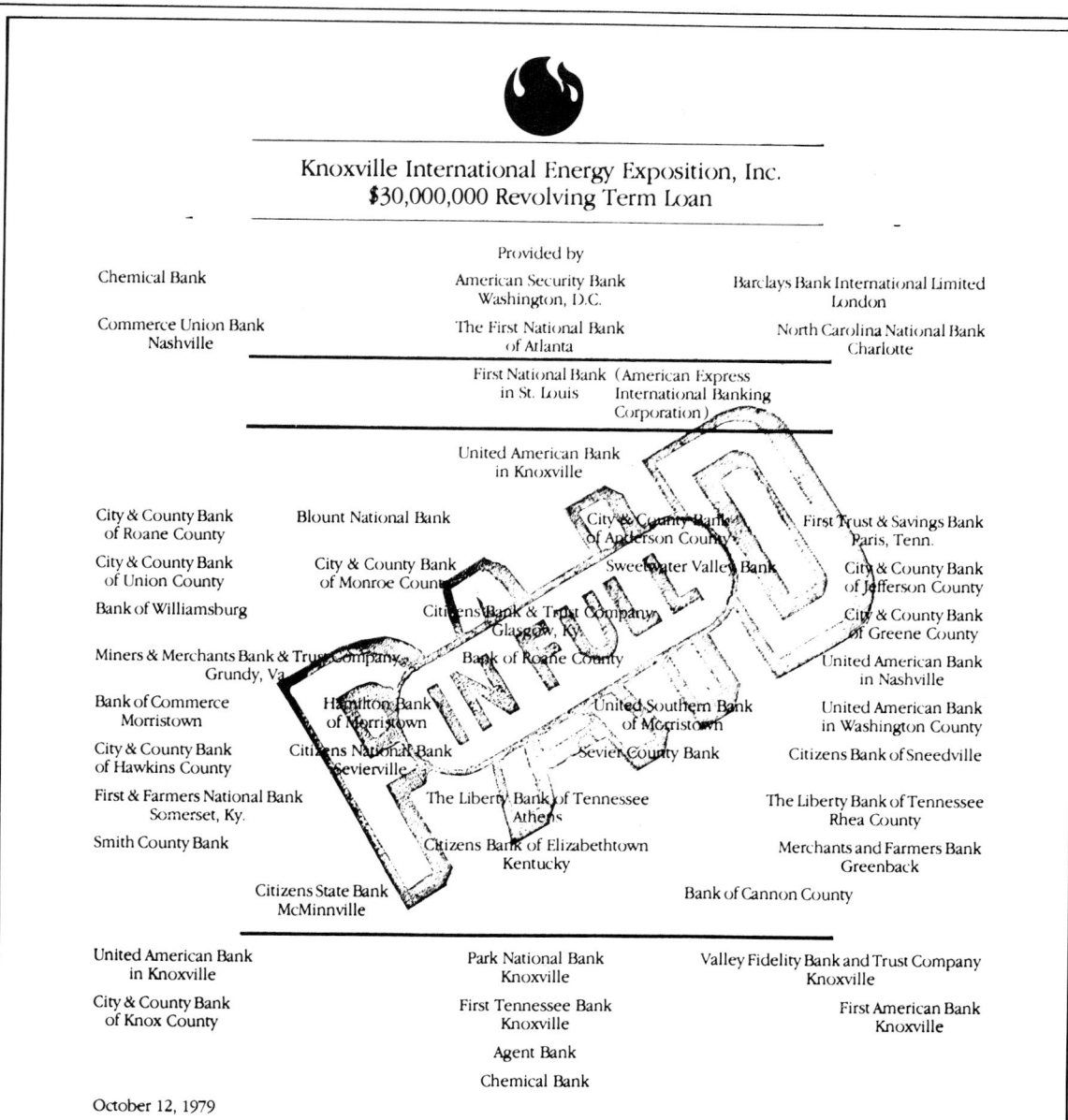

The Second Creek Valley, an unsightly area of abandoned railroad tracks and dilapidated buildings, had been targeted by the city of Knoxville for urban renewal. The 1982 World's Fair was an interim use of the cleared site, and the Fair was financed with a $30,000,000 line of credit provided by a consortium of forty-five banks. That loan was repaid in full two weeks before the Fair closed, and copies of the cancelled debt were given to guests at the note-burning ceremony. Author's Collection

While the 1982 World's Fair was in the planning stages, this table-top scale-model of the site was exhibited to stimulate local interest and encourage business participation. Greater Knoxville Chamber of Commerce

Before the Knoxville Iron Works moved to Lonsdale in 1901, it was located in the Second Creek Valley. The large building with the cupola, its original foundry, was built at the end of the Civil War; it took a new lease on life in 1982 when it was transformed into the Strohhaus. McClung Historical Collection

The Louisville and Nashville Railroad Station, completed in 1906, boasted stained-glass windows and tiled floors laid in oriental carpet patterns. The Ladies Waiting Room, featuring a separate entrance and a fireplace, was furnished in oak with a massive library table, writing desks, and rocking chairs.

In preparation for Expo '82, the abandoned station's patterned floors were repaired and its missing stained glass panes were replaced with locally-made exact replicas of the originals. The L&N still houses two popular restaurants that opened with the Fair. The distinctive roof of the Foundry/Strohhaus appears in the background of this photograph of the Station undergoing restoration. Knoxville Convention and Visitors Bureau

The Littlefield & Steere Candy Company's multi-story building at the western end of the Clinch Avenue Viaduct was revamped to offer multiple food services and craft sales; the closed viaduct, lined with shops, served as a pedestrian walkway to the Candy Factory, which became the temporary home of the Knoxville Art Museum in 1987. Knoxville News-Sentinel

UNITED STATES PAVILION—NORTHWEST VIEW
1982 KNOXVILLE INTERNATIONAL ENERGY EXPOSITION

The design for the $12,000,000 United States Pavilion, which won a national architectural competition, called for the building to be entered from the top by means of outside escalators. During the Fair, the Pavilion was a sprightly showcase, but retrofitting it for adaptive use turned out to be prohibitively expensive.

Everything was in readiness on May 1, 1982, when President Ronald Reagan officially opened the first World's Fair in the southeastern United States. This aerial view, taken from a Police helicopter, shows the Fair's first visitors streaming through the gates. Nearby parking lots remained half empty, because most of the eighty thousand opening day visitors arrived by bus — chartered-tour, private-shuttle, or public-transit.

Before the gates closed for the last time on October 31, the Fair's attendance totalled a record-breaking 11,127,786. Knoxville Police Department

The Peruvian Pavilion displayed Inca mummy-bundles, plus $43,000,000 worth of pre-Columbian gold. Egypt offered an overview of five thousand years of civilization. Life-size clay funerary figures, unearthed after two thousand years from an emperor's tomb, high-lighted the China Pavilion. Photographs by Betsey Creekmore

Treasures of Antiquity from around the World

Electricity helped East Tennessee's gentle breezes power Australia's giant mobile of spinning windmills. Photograph by Betsey Creekmore

The walking, talking catsup bottle handed out free pickle pins. Photograph by Betsey Creekmore

Funland, featuring the world's largest Ferris wheel, occupied the Thompson-Boling Arena site. A temporary bridge across Neyland Drive provided access to TVA's floating exhibit, built on twin barges by retirees. Tennessee Valley Authority

These "plaster persons" on the TVA barge represented East Tennesseans who lined up to apply for jobs at Norris Dam in 1933. Tennessee Valley Authority

An overhead tram line called Sky-Tanspo carried foot-sore fairgoers from one end of the site to the other. Author's Collection

The Technology and Lifestyle Center, where children of all ages lined up to see the amazingly detailed Miniature Circus, reopened immediately after the Fair as the city's Exhibition Center. Knoxville Convention and Visitors Bureau

Two of the Fair's most unusual structures—the Sunsphere, and the Tennessee Amphitheatre—remain. *Knoxville Convention and Visitors Bureau*

"The summer of 1982 was a happy time!" *Final Report of the United States Commissioner General for the Knoxville International Energy Exposition—ENERGY EXPO '82—to the President of the United States*

We love to join in!

Wall-to-wall people on Gay Street, enjoying Saturday Night on the Town in 1983. The Lamar House/Bijou, restored by Knoxville Heritage, Inc., is at the left. East Tennessee Community Design Center

Through the years, Blount Mansion's guests have come by carriage and by car. But more than eleven hundred came by trolley for First Night Fest in 1986. City of Knoxville Information Office

Since 1982, the annual Expo 10,000 has filled Gay Street with runners, curb to curb. Knoxville Convention and Visitors Bureau

A statewide project of Tennessee Homecoming '86 was the creation of this mammoth quilt, in which each of the ninety-five counties is represented by an intricate appliqued square. Knox County's square is fifth from the top, in the left hand row.

Gov. Lamar Alexander, who originated the year-long Homecoming, celebrated Statehood Day on June 1 by unveiling the quilt on the grounds of Blount Mansion in Knoxville, Tennessee's first capital.
Knoxville News-Sentinel

This is Knoxville—founded in 1791 as America's first territorial capital; the home of The University of Tennessee, chartered as Blount College by the nation's first territorial legislature in 1794; the first capital of the state of Tennessee, 1796-1811; the only city that withstood a Civil War siege, 1863; site of the first National Conservation Exposition, 1913; since 1926, the gateway to the Great Smoky Mountains National Park; since 1933, the headquarters of the Tennessee Valley Authority, and now encircled by six of TVA's Great Lakes of the South; host city of the 1982 World's Fair, the first in the southeastern United States. Photograph by Gary Heatherly

BIBLIOGRAPHY

Bowman, Elizabeth Skaggs and Folmsbee, Stanley J. "The Ramsey House." Reprint, Knoxville: East Tennessee Historical Society, 1965.

Brownlow, William G. *Parson Brownlow's Book.* Philadelphia: George W. Childs, 1862

City of Knoxville Tennessee (Illustrated). Knoxville: Board of Trade, 1905.

"Civil War Monuments and Memorials in Tennessee." Nashville: Civil War Centennial Commission, 1963.

Commercial History of the State of Tennessee. Chattanooga: Travelers' Protective Association of America, 1910.

Creekmore, Betsey Beeler. *Knoxville.* Third Edition. Knoxville: The University of Tennessee Press, 1976.

____. *Knoxville, Our Fair City.* Knoxville: Greater Knoxville Chamber of Commerce, 1984.

Deaderick, Lucille, (Ed.). *Heart of the Valley.* Knoxville: East Tennessee Historical Society, 1976.

"50th Anniversary, The Great Smoky Mountains National Park." National Park Service, 1985.

"The Future of Our Past." (Historic Sites Survey). Knoxville: Knoxville/Knox County Metropolitan Planning Commission, 1987.

Gilchrist, Annie S. *Some Representative Women of Tennessee.* Nashville, 1902.

Goodman, W.M. *Knoxville, The Marble City.* Knoxville, c. 1900.

Hicks, Nannie Lee. "Historic Treasure Spots of Knox County, Tennessee." Knoxville: Simon Harris Chapter, Daughters of the American Revolution, 1964.

____. "The John Adair Section of Knox County, Tennessee." Knoxville, 1968.

"Historical Forts and Houses in Knoxville and Nearby Vicinity." Knoxville: Knox County Library, 1962.

History of Homes and Gardens of Tennessee. Nashville: Garden Study Club of Nashville, 1936.

History of Tennessee. (East Tennessee Edition). Nashville: Goodspeed Publishing Company, 1887.

Knox County in the World War. Knoxville: Knoxville Lithographing Company, 1919.

"Knoxville, Fifty Landmarks." Knoxville: Junior League of Knoxville, 1976.

Knoxville Heritage, Inc. tour brochures: "Mechanicsville and Knoxville College," 1981; "Historic Fort Sanders," 1981; "Kingston Pike-Lyons View," 1984.

McAdoo, William G. *Crowded Years.* Boston: Houghton Miflin Company, 1931.

McGee, Gentry R. *History of Tennessee.* Jackson, 1947.

McNabb, William Ross, (Ed.). "Architecture in Knoxville, Tennessee, 1790-1940." Knoxville: Dulin Gallery of Art and McClung Historical Collection, 1974.

Morse, Charles R, (Ed.). *The University of Tennessee Magazine, Historical Edition.* Knoxville, 1920.

Poe, Orlando M. "Occupation of East Tennessee and the Defense of Knoxville." Reprint, Knoxville: East Tennessee Historical Society, 1963.

Ramsey, J.G.M. *The Annals of Tennessee to the End of the Eighteenth Century.* Charleston: Walker and James, 1853.

____. "History of Lebanon Presbyterian Church," 1875. Reprint, Knoxville: Hubert Hodge Printing Company, 1973.

Rothrock, Mary U., (Ed.). *The French-Broad Holston Country.* Knoxville: East Tennessee Historical Society, 1946.

____. *This is Tennessee.* Knoxville, 1963.

Rule, William, (Ed.). *Standard History of Knoxville, Tennessee.* Chicago: Lewis Publishing Company, 1900.

Scott, Edith. *The Story of Two Chairs.* (A Fairytale That is Truer Than False). Bristol, 1957.

Timberlake, Henry. *Memoirs, 1756-1765.* Watauga Press, 1927

INDEX

A
Abrams Falls, 73
Acacia Rose Circle, 39
Adair, John, 85
advertising fan, 46
Agee, James, 144
Agricultural Experiment Station, 76
Alcoa Highway, 78, 79
America's first coeds, 24, 115, 148-149, 153
Andrew Johnson Hotel, 215-216
Appalachian Exposition(s), 35-36, 37, 40
Armstrong houses on Kingston Pike, 120-121
Armstrong, Jenny, 148, 149
Arnstein Building, 201
Atkin birthday party, 209
Atkin, C. B., 196, 209
atomic reactor, 131
Austin-East Jazz Band, 46
Australian Pavilion, 79, 229
Ayres, Dr. Brown, 155, 198
Ayres Hall, 155

B
Ballet Benefit, 98
bandstand, Chilhowee Park, 40
Baptist Hospital, 81, 202
Battle of Campbell's Station, 118
Battle of Fort Sanders, 119, 143
Belcaro, 98-99
Bell House, The (School), 217
Berry, Ellen McClung, 22, 99
Beverly Hills Sanitarium, 107
Bicentennial, U.S., 40, 57, 125, 204
Bijou Theatre, 200, 233
Bleak House, 121
Blockhouse Fort, 112, 172
Blount College, 18, 24, 85, 115, 146-150, 153, 196, 212
Blount mansion, 17, 141, 148, 168-169, 171, 173, 233
Blount, Gov. William, 16-17, 53, 137, 146, 148, 165-166, 168, 169, 170-173
Bonny Kate Chapter, DAR, 28, 116, 141, 210
Branner family, 33
Branson, Lloyd, 18, 23, 172, 191
Briscoe, Daniel, Sr. (house), 138
Briscoe, Russell, 96, 141, 178
Brownlow, William G., 30, 176, 179, 180
buffalo, 10, 11
Burnett, Frances Hodgson, 91
Burnside, Gen. Ambrose, 177
Burwell Building, 196

C
Cal Johnson City Park, 47
Callahan, George W. (house), 109
Campbell's Station, 113, 118, 136
Candy Factory, 225
Cantilevered barn, 14-15
Carl Cowan Park, 133
Carnegie Library, 45
Carrick, Elizabeth M., 21
Carrick, Reverend Samuel, 18, 21
Catholic High School, 33
Catsup bottle robot, 229
Cavett's Station, 112
Central High School, 97
Chamber of Commerce, 182
Chapman, David, 71
Chapman Highway, 71, 74, 75
Cherokee Bridge, 76
Cherokee Country Club, 128, 129
Cherokee Indians, 11-17, 19, 21, 53, 57, 81, 85, 88, 112, 114, 124, 126, 127, 165, 166, 172
Chesterfield, 25
Chilhowee Park, 34-42, 43
Chimneys, The, 72
China Pavilion, 228
Chisholm's Tavern, 171
Christy, Howard Chandler, 15
Church of the Immaculate Conception, 180
Church Street United Methodist Church, 212
Circle Park, 160
circus parade, 190
City/County Building, 220
City Hall, 179, 182, 220
city watertower, 44
civic auditorium (early), 199
Civic Auditorium/Coliseum, 48-49, 50
Civil War, 60-61, 90, 92, 117, 118-119, 121, 137, 138, 143, 176-181, 186
Civil War Centennial, 60
Clarence Brown Theatre, 163
Clinch River, 17, 110, 131
coeds of 1893, 153
Cole-Harris house, 87
Commerce Avenue Fire Hall, 206
Concord Park, 133
Confederate Army, 44, 60-61, 92, 118-119, 150, 176-177, 179
Confederate Cemetery, 31
Confederate Memorial Hall, 121
Constitutional Convention of Tennessee, 85, 173
Country music, 203

Cowan, James D. (house), 138
Cowan, McClung & Company, 187
Craighead-Jackson House, 171
Creek Indians, 87, 112, 172
Crescent Bend, 99, 120
Custom House, 204, 205

D
dairying, 76, 89
Davis, Mrs. W. P., 71
Dead Horse Lake, 130
Delaney, Joseph, 46
Dickinson, Col. Perez, 62-63, 178, 209
Dickinson's Island, 62, 64
Dogwood Arts Festival, 97, 193
Dogwood Trail(s), 43, 75, 80, 97, 127, 129
dugout canoe, 57, 85
Dulin Gallery of Art, 123
dummy line, the, 95
Dumplin Creek, Treaty of, 14, 19, 53
Dunn, J. M. (house), 101

E
early explorers, 12, 13, 14, 19, 22, 85, 113, 165
East Tennessee, 11-14, 165
East Tennessee Female Institute, 212
East Tennessee Historical Center, 204
East Tennessee Insane Asylum, 128
East Tennessee University, 61, 150-152
Egyptian Pavilion, 228
Eleventh Street Artists' Colony, 145
Ellis & Ernest Drugstore, 160
Emory Road, 85, 109
Energy Expo '82, 221-232
Estabrook Hall, 152, 161
Expo 10,000, 234
Exposition Buildings, Chilhowee Park, 35-40

F
Farragut, Adm. David G., 35, 116-117, 197
Farragut, 118, 136
Farragut High School, 36
ferryboat, 65
Fireman's Statue, 213
first airplane, 35
First Baptist Church, 208
First Creek, 16, 17, 50, 165, 178
First Presbyterian Church, 18, 85, 172
first territorial capital, 17, 165, 169, 173
Flanagan-Goddard house, 54
flat-tops (housing), 131, 157
flatboats, 57, 58

Forks of the Rivers, 13, 15, 19, 20, 22, 23
Fort Adair, 84, 85
Fort Dickerson, 60
Fort Loudoun, 12-13
Fort Loudoun Dam, 82, 132
Fort Loudoun Lake, 132-135
Fort Sanders, 60, 119, 121, 137, 138, 143, 150
Fort Sanders Hospital, 60, 143
Fort Sanders Neighborhood, 137, 143-145
Fouché building, 178
Fountain City, 34, 85, 94-97
Fourth & Gill Neighborhood, 103
Fourth of July parade, 189
Fox, Reuben (house), 91
Frank H. McClung Museum, 57, 148
Franklin, Lost State of, 14-15, 19, 53
Fraternity Park, 161
French Broad River, 13, 15, 17, 19, 20, 53, 56, 58, 60, 168
frontier costumes, 55
Fulton, Weston M. (house), 129
Funland, 230

G
Gay Street, 44, 146, 178, 186-203, 214-219, 233, 234
Gay Street Bridge(s), 60, 66
Gay Street Fire, 186-187
Gay Street houses, 214
Gay/Way, 188
Gibbs, Nicholas, 86
Glenmary, 115
golf course(s), 43, 106, 128
Governor Blount's office, 17, 166, 169, 170
Grainger, Mary E., 148, 149
Grassy Valley, 14, 15, 113, 116, 136
great iron chain, 60
Great Lakes of the South, 132, 235
Great Seal of Tennessee, 57
Great Smoky Mountains National Park, 71-74, 235
Greenwood, Albert (house), 102
Greystone, 101

H
Haley, Alex (house), 125
Halloween high jinx, 155
Halls, 109, 193
Hardin Valley, 113, 137
Harris, Simon, 87
Hastie, Judge William, 69
Hayes, President Rutherford B., 30, 200
Heiskell, Frederick S., 89, 114
Henley Street Bridge, 81, 82, 173
Heska Amuna Synagogue, 31
Hiroshima West, 160
Hodges Ferry, 65
Holbrook College, 97
Holston Hills, 43
Holston River, 13, 17, 19, 20, 21, 24, 43, 58, 85
Holston, Treaty of, 16-17, 53, 165
Hope, Thomas, 22, 24, 114, 162
Hopecote, 162
horsedrawn streetcar(s), 102, 190
Hoskins, Dr. James D., 152
Hospital rules, 179

House Mountain, 20
House-Hasson envelope, 36
Houston, Sam, 88
Howell Nurseries, 43
Humes, Dr. Thomas W., 150
Hurst, Edward, 148
Hyatt-Regency Hotel, 51

I
I. C. King Park, 79
ice-skating rink, 185
Ijams, Harry P., 63
Ijams-Audubon Nature Center, 64
Indian boundary, 13, 15, 53
Indian massacre(s), 13, 52, 53, 87, 112, 114
Indian Mound(s), 125, 151
Indian towns, 11, 12, 16, 85, 165
Ish, John, 52, 53, 54
Island Home, 62-63

J
Jackson, President Andrew, 30
Jackson Avenue warehouses, 186
James White's house, 16, 50, 70, 166-167
James White marker(s), 28
John C. Hodges Library, 163
John Sevier Monument, 214
Johnson, Calvin F., 35, 47
Johnson Bible College, 68

K
Kain, Mattie and Kittie, 24, 149
Karns, 91
Keener-Hunt house, 59
Kennedy, James, Jr., 166-167
Kennedy, James, Sr., 30
Kimberlin Heights, 53, 68
Kingston Pike, 76, 113, 114, 118, 120-121, 124, 140, 178
Knaffl Madonna, 162
Knox, Major General Henry, 17, 164, 165
Knox County, founding of, 17, 169
Knox County Court, 113, 201
Knox County Courthouse, 172, 213, 214, 220
Knox County flag, 57
Knoxville, founding of, 17, 165-166, 167
Knoxville College, 91-93
Knoxville Cookbook, 198
Knoxville General Hospital, 104
Knoxville High School, 103
Knoxville Iron Company, 108, 224
Knoxville Sentinel, 201
Knoxville Symphony, 48, 197
Krutch Park, 205

L
L&N Station, 224
Lake Ottosee, 32-34
Lamar House (hotel), 200, 233
Land Grant College(s), 92, 151
Lawson McGhee (Williams), 207
Lawson McGhee Library, 192, 207
Lebanon-in-the-Fork Church, 18, 21, 85
Legg-England stagecoach inn, 25
Lincoln Memorial Hospital, 104
Little Diamond, 42
Little River, 14, 53, 54, 56
livestock parade, 189

Lockett, A. Percy (house), 211
Longstreet, Gen. James, 119, 121, 179
Longstreet's Heights, 61
Lonsdale, 108
Louis Philippe, Duc d'Orleans, 169
Lyceum building, 210
Lyons View, 128

M
Mabry, Joseph A., Jr., 44, 181
McAdoo, William Gibbs, 32, 86
McBee's fruitstand, 45
McCammon, Samuel (house), 28
McClung, C. J., 122, 208
McClung, Charles, 17, 113, 114-115, 148
McClung, Polly, 115, 148
McClure family portrait, 159
McGhee Tyson Airport, 78, 140
McMillan, Edward J. (house), 158
Magnolia Avenue, 33
Main Street houses, 210
Manefee, John, 14, 85
Mann, George, 87
Maple Bend, 56
Maplehurst, 211
Maps:
  Cherokee towns, 12
  Civil War defenses, 178
  East Knox County, 21
  North Knox County, 86
  South Knox County, 54
  West Knox County, 114
  Knox County boundaries, 16
  Tennessee in 1796, 173
marble quarry, 23
Marble Springs Plantation, 55
Market House, 181, 182-184
Market Square, 44, 181-185
Mascot, 26-27
Mason, James, 29
Mechanicsville, 93
Melrose, 138, 141
Melton Hill Lake, 132, 135
Methodist campground, 94
Michaux, André, 169
Middlebrook, 117
military hospital(s), 172, 176, 178, 179
moon-rocks bag, 83
moonshine still, 70
Mount Rest Home, 27
Mountain Lion Fountain, 126

N
National Cemetery, 90
National Conservation Exposition, 37-40
Neubert Springs gazebo, 68
Newcomer's department store, 188
Neyland Stadium, 161
Norris Dam, 17, 109, 110
Norris Freeway, 109
North Carolina, 11, 12, 13-15, 19, 85, 165
North Knoxville, 105, 111

O
Oak Ridge, 131, 157
Oakwood, 122
Old City Hall, 220
Old College, 150, 155
Old Gray Cemetery, 90
Old North Knoxville, 100-101

Old Sevierville Pike, 59, 67
Omnibuggy, the, 67
Ossoli Circle, 141, 210

P
pack horses, 84, 168
paddlewheel steamer(s), 58
Papoose Park, 126-127
Peale, Charles Willson, 174
pedal cars, 212
Pellissippi, 136, 137
pencil portraits in the tower, 121
Peruvian Pavilion, 228
Peter Blow place, 77
planetarium, 41
Plaza Tower, 219
Post Office, 210
Powell, 85, 88
Promenade Block, 188
protest march, 156
pullman cars, 195
pumping station, 44
puppet show, 232

R
race track(s), 35, 47, 118
Racheff Gardens, 108
Ramsey, Dr. J. G. M., 23
Ramsey, Francis Alexander, 14, 19, 22-23, 113
Ramsey, Margaret Russell, 22
Ramsey, Reverend S. G., 113, 115
Reagan, President Ronald, 227
Red Cross Canteen, 194
Renault limousine, 183
Revolutionary War, 13, 87, 164, 168
Rich's/Miller's/Hess's, 203
Riverview Towers, 217
Roane, Governor Archibald, 116
Ronald McDonald House, 144
Roosevelt, President Franklin D., 110, 156
Roosevelt, President Theodore, 30, 199
Ross, M. L., 143, 213
Russell, Avery, 118
Ryan, Father Abram Joseph, 180

S
S&W Cafeteria, 202
Sanders, General William P., 121
Sanford Arboretum, 124
Santa Claus Parade, 193
Saturday Night on the Town, 233
Scott, Colonel Joseph, 99, 120
Scott, Francis A. R., 100
Sequoyah, 124
Sequoyah Hills, 124-127
Seven Islands, 56
Sevier, Governor John, 13, 14-15, 19, 53, 55, 174-175, 214
Sevier-Park House, 175
Sharp's Ridge Park, 111
Shields-Watkins field, 157
shipping channel, 82-83
Shrine parade, 188
Siege of Knoxville, 179, 204
Sky-Transpo, 231
solar houses, 79
South College, 152
Southern Railway, 24, 105, 111, 194-195

souvenir plate, 81
Soviet Sports Exhibition, 220
Spanish-American War Parade, 191
Speedwell, 77
St. John's Episcopal Church, 175
St. Mary's Hospital, 95, 107
Statesview, 114, 148
Staub's Opera House, 218
Sterchi, J. G. (house), 89
streetcar Barn, 199
Strohhaus, 224
Summer School of the South, 154
Sunnyside, 137, 148
Sunsphere, 232

T
TVA barge exhibit, 230
TVA lakes, 13, 132-135, 235
TVA system, 82-83
TVA towers, 206
TVA's first directors, 156
tabletop model(s), 153, 173, 222-223
Talahi, 126-127
Taylor, Judge George C. (house), 123
Technology and Lifestyle Center, 231
Temple, Mary Boyce, 141, 170
Tennessee Amphitheatre, 232
Tennessee Centennial, 153, 198
Tennessee Homecoming quilt, 235
Tennessee River, 13, 16, 20, 53, 58, 60-61, 62, 65, 76-77, 82, 113, 133, 165
Tennessee School for the Deaf, 29, 62-63, 176, 179, 220
Tennessee Terrace Hotel, 214-215
Tennessee Theatre, 196-197
Tennessee Valley Authority (TVA), 13, 17, 82-83, 132-135, 156, 204-206, 235
Tennessee Volunteers, 13, 157
Tennessee's first capital, 173, 174, 235
Territorial capital, 17, 165-166, 169, 173, 235
Territorial capitol, 166, 169
Territory South of the River Ohio, 15, 16, 165-166, 169, 173
The Hill, 137, 150-157, 160, 161
Thomas/McClung cousins, 122
Thompson-Boling Arena, 163, 230
Timberlake, Lieutenant Henry, 12
Todd & Armistead Drugstore, 202
Trafalgar, 24, 149, 162
traffic control, 201
trolley car(s), 32, 199, 233
Tudor house of railroad ties, 130
Tyson, Bettie McGhee, 140, 198
Tyson, Lawrence D., 139, 191
Tyson House, 138-140, 163
Tyson Park, 140

U
US 11 E, 24
US 11 W, 25
U.S. Pavilion, 225
UT cadets, 151, 152, 191, 198
UT Farm, 76, 78, 151
UT Hospital, 78
Union Academy, 88
Union forces, Civil War, 23, 44, 60, 90, 118-119, 121, 150, 176-179, 181
United States Constitution, 15, 168
University of Tennessee, 150, 152-163, 191, 198
Urban Renewal, 47-51, 158-161, 221

V
Vestal, 67
Viaduct, Gay Street, 105, 195
Victory Parade, 1899, 191
Virginia, 12, 13, 19, 24, 25, 53, 85, 113, 178
Volunteer State, the, 13

W
WATE-TV, 101
WNOX Radio Station, 106, 203
wallpaper, French scenic, 99, 120
Washington, Booker T., parade, 39
Washington, President George, 15, 16, 164
watersports, 133-135
We love a parade!, 189-193
We love to join in!, 233-235
Westmoreland waterwheel, 129
Westwood, 121
Wheeler wedding party, 46
White's Fort, 16, 28, 50, 165
White, James, 16, 17, 19, 20, 28, 29, 50, 113, 115, 165-167
Wholesale houses, 186-187
Williams, John (house), 29
Wilson, President Woodrow, 32, 86
Woman's Building, 198-199
Wooddale, 24
Woodruff, W. W., 142, 187
World War I, 192, 194
World War II, 78, 131, 157
World's Fair Site, 145, 221, 222-223
World's Fair, 1982, 79, 221-232

Z
Zoo, the Knoxville, 42

239

About The Author

Betsey Beeler Creekmore was born in 1915, in a house on Gay Street which faced the Knox County Courthouse. A 1935 graduate of Vassar College, she is a member of Phi Beta Kappa. As a lifelong resident of Knox County, she has experienced at first hand the impact of the Great Smoky Mountains National Park, TVA's Great Lakes of the South, Oak Ridge, and the 1982 World's Fair. She is active in business and civic affairs; is the author of eleven previous books, two of which, *Knoxville,* and *Knoxville, Our Fair City* also deal with local history; and is the originator of Knoxville's annual Dogwood Trails and their outgrowth, the Dogwood Arts Festival.

She was married in 1938 to Frank B. Creekmore, an attorney, and is the mother of twins, David and Betsey.

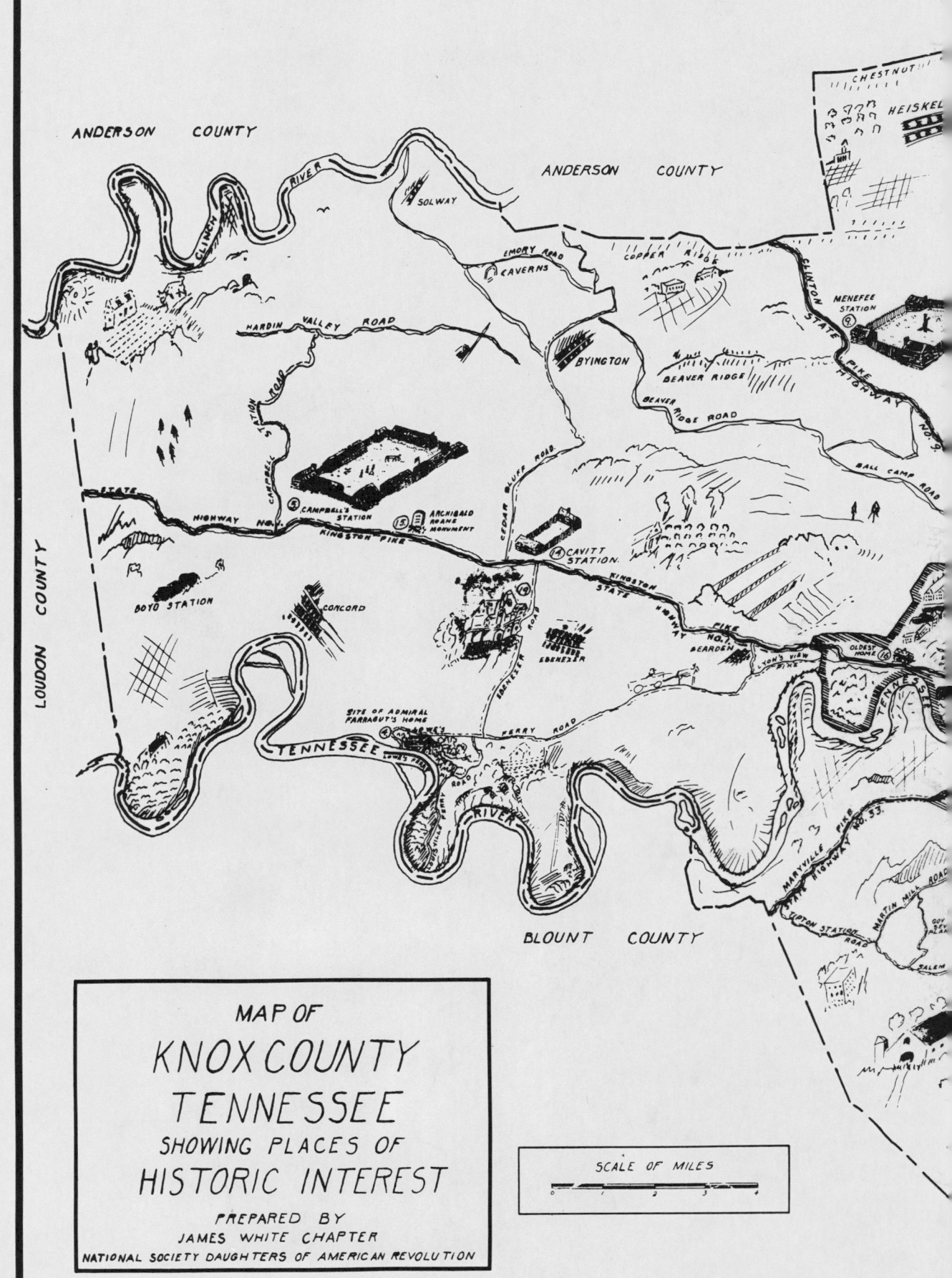

CARDS

DATE DUE			
AUG 1X 1989			
FEB 5 1991			
DEC 23 1993			
DEC 16 1995			

UPPER CUMBERLAND
REGIONAL LIBRARY CENTER
Cookeville, Tennessee